GATHERING
—ISRAEL—
How Great Shall Be
YOUR JOY

Gary J. Coleman

DIGITAL
LEGEND

© 2022 by Digital Legend Press

Without limiting the rights under copyright above, no part of this publication may be reproduced, stored in or introduced into a retrieval system,
or transmitted, in any form, or by any means (electronic, mechanical, photocopying, recording, or use in motion pictures and otherwise), without the prior written permission of the publisher of this book.

Published by
Digital Legend Press & Publishing, Inc.
Salt Lake City, UT
www.digitalegend.com
info@digitalegend.com
801-810-7718

ISBN: 978-1-934537-81-7

Permission was granted by the Office of the First Presidency to author in writing to publish this book.

This work is not an official publication of The Church of Jesus Christ of Latter-day Saints. The views expressed herein are the responsibility of the author and do not necessarily represent the position of the Church.

Printed in the United States of America

Cover layout by: Boyd J Tuttle

Cover Image: depiction of a sheaf of wheat, emblem of Joseph's tribe, with its Hebrew name יוֹסֵף (Yosefu) which is located in the HaPoel HaMizrachi Central synagogue in Bnei Brak, Israel.

Interior design and layout by: Jacob F. Frandsen

*To all those who seek the beautiful truths
of the restored gospel of Jesus Christ*

*And in special tribute to Judith Renée England Coleman,
my beloved wife, through whom the Lord brought me
this glorious message.*

*I express my appreciation to Jennifer Reidhead
for her assistance in typing the manuscript.*

Contents

Preface

Elder Gary J. Coleman, a convert to The Church of Jesus Christ of Latter-day Saints, has set his course in life on helping gather the children of Israel to the Restored Gospel of Jesus Christ and has exemplified the true meaning of Gathering Israel and "How "Great Will Be Your Joy!"

Through the years Elder Coleman, by his example, and in his writing and doctrinal messages, has provided a means for how everyone seeking to know the truth of life and salvation can find it in the doctrines of The Church of Jesus Christ of Latter-day Saints. Implicit in his words is the promise that seekers of truth who pursue a course of study, who ponder and ultimately ask in faith, will gain a testimony of the gospel's truth and divinity.

His book "Great Will Be Your Joy!" serves as an instructional witness for individuals and families to find the peace and happiness depicted in the gospel, as taught and lived by Jesus the Christ.

Prophets since the beginning of time have counseled those who have found the truth to share it with neighbors and friends. Elder Coleman provides simple ways to become acquainted with them, share a copy of the Book of Mormon and your feelings about a specific principle or doctrine, and ask if the missionaries can teach them.

To those who may have strayed from the Church, the testimonies inherent in his writings will help them have a deepening desire to someday return.

The invitation is for each of us to be instrumental in providing the way and receiving the joy that comes in bringing souls unto Christ.

—V. Daniel Rogers, former 40 years instructor and administrator in Church Education System

Introduction

Elder Dieter F. Uchtdorf, Apostle of the Lord Jesus Christ, recently said in a virtual missionary worldwide devotional, "You missionaries have been called, set apart and commissioned to assist the Savior and living Apostles in this great work." "You are to interact with people in normal and natural ways." You are to "serve and minister to others, helping Church members in their efforts to come and help, come and see, and come and belong." Thus we are all "called to serve and share the good news of the restored gospel of Jesus Christ with all people and nations" (*Church News*, August 16, 2020).

We have called this "Member Missionary Work" for many decades of our Church history. This process and effort to serve as full-time and member missionaries actually started in April 1829 at Fayette, New York and was to be "relative to building up the Church," with the Church actually being organized in 1830. Note the following seven verses from Section 18 of the Doctrine and Covenants:

"10 *Remember the worth of souls is great in the sight of God;*
11 *For, behold, the Lord your Redeemer suffered death in the flesh; wherefore he suffered the pain of all men, that all men might repent and come unto him.*

12 *And he hath risen again from the dead, that he might bring all men unto him, on conditions of repentance.*

13 *And how great is his joy in the soul that repenteth!*

14 *Wherefore, you are called to cry repentance unto this people.* 15 *And if it so be that you should labor all your days in crying repentance unto this people, and bring, save it be one soul unto me, how great shall be your joy with him in the kingdom of my Father!*

16 *And now, if your joy will be great with one soul that you have brought unto me into the kingdom of my Father, how great will be your joy if you should bring many souls unto me!*

17 *Behold, you have my gospel before you, and my rock, and my salvation."*

Thus the subtitle of my book: *How Great Shall Be Your Joy!"*

I will testify over and over again about the evidence I have witnessed of *"the worth of souls is great in the sight of God."* I will testify again and again about the joy of the Savior in the "soul that repenteth," and the joy of all of us to "bring, save it be one soul unto me and how <u>great</u> shall be your joy with him in the kingdom of my Father." I will testify from dozens and dozens of personal experiences in my own life as to the blessing of "your (my) joy will be great with one soul that you hath brought unto me into the kingdom of my Father, how great will be your (my) joy if you should bring many souls unto me" (Doctrine and Covenants 18:10-16).

I have learned over my lifetime, now 60 years as an adult convert to The Church of Jesus Christ of Latter-day Saints that the Lord truly does not fault our efforts to "invite them in as converts" or "invite them back" by re-activation!

Does religion have any relevance today? Is there a religion that answers our many questions about life and death? What does one do in a religious dilemma? I was faced with one such dilemma as I became aware of many inconsistencies between the Biblical scriptures and the practices of my church. Though I had attempted to worship God all my life, I still could not feel a closeness to a God who was defined as being "incomprehensible." I looked into my worship experience and found it rote, ancient, and stagnant.

Modern revelation was not a teaching of my church. The only mention of prophets was to revere those of the ancient records. I

INTRODUCTION

had been taught that to hope for or anticipate a prophet in my day
was to seek a false prophet.

I had planned all of my early life to become a Priest. The closer
I drew to committing my life to the training within a theological
seminary, the more I sought for some glimmer of peace within my
religion.

I met a person who said that she belonged to The Church of
Jesus Christ of Latter-day Saints, the only true Church upon the
face of the earth. All my life I had been taught that my church was
the only true church. How could more than one church claim such
a position? Being on the brink of a discovery, I became acquainted
with the Latter-day Saints, more formally referred to as members
of The Church of Jesus Christ of Latter-day Saints. They introduced
me to a way of life that has penetrated every fiber of my being.

May I share with you some things that I have learned in the
past few years about this most unusual religion? I would like to
discuss a few of the feelings that have sunk deep into my heart as
I have come to know about the true gospel of Jesus Christ. Who
would have ever guessed that this Church holds the keys to truths
and knowledge that many have never tapped? This is a missionary
Church. We are all to assist the Lord as members of the Church.

In 1978, I completed a doctoral dissertation called "Member
Missionary Involvement in the LDS Church" at Brigham Young
University, under the direction of the Missionary Department of
the Church. Many of the thoughts expressed in this book are based
upon the research and findings of that study. In those days of over
40 years ago, there were approximately 30,000 full-time missionaries serving among a Church population of just over four million
members. In recent years we have seen the number of missionaries in the fields of labor swell to 60 and 70 and 80,000. The Church
membership has also grown to over 16 million as of the April
2020 General Conference report. In addition, numerous personal
experiences associated with member missionary work since my
conversion to The Church of Jesus Christ of Latter-day Saints have
taught me principles that are functional and applicable to a variety
of missionary circumstances. Nineteen eighty-seven was the peak

year for baptisms in the Church. From 1988-2019 baptisms trended downward worldwide though missionaries serving had doubled and membership in the Church overall had quadrupled. Missionaries need the help and influence and time and support of members in this vast undertaking of participating in the joy the Lord seeks and He shares with us when we bring more souls unto Him.

The word "joy" is used multiple times in the Lord's scriptures. Joy is also associated with the scriptural terms of "joyful," "rejoice," "joyous," and "gladness." We read of the following expressions related to joy: "Many shouted aloud for joy," "all the sons of God shouted for joy," "my soul shall be joyful in the Lord," "Everlasting joy shall be upon their heads," "enter thou into the joy of the Lord," "good (glad) tidings of great joy," "rejoice, because your names are written in heaven," "that your joy may be full," "men are that they might have joy." It is delightful to see that the joy we seek in the Lord and His great plan for us is truly an unfathomed joy for everyone. (See Appendix VI for the use of the word "joy" in the *Hymnbook of The Church of Jesus Christ of Latter-day Saints.*)

In his first General Conference as President of The Church of Jesus Christ of Latter-day Saints, April 2018, President Russell M. Nelson said, "Our message to the world is simple and sincere: we invite all of God's children on both sides of the veil to come unto their Savior, receive the blessings of the holy temple, have enduring joy, and qualify for eternal life."

He further said, "I bless you to raise your voice in testimony, as I do now, that we are engaged in the work of Almighty God! Jesus is the Christ. This is His Church, which He directs through His anointed servants" (Russell M. Nelson, "Let Us All Press On," *Ensign,* May 2018).

More recently President Nelson has added, "This pre-millennial gathering is an individual saga of expanding faith and spiritual courage for millions of people. And, as members of The Church of Jesus Christ of Latter-day Saints, or "latter-day covenant Israel," we have been charged to assist the Lord with this pivotal work... Anytime we do anything that helps anyone—on either side of the veil—to make and keep their covenants with God we are helping to gather Israel" (*Church News*, Oct 10, 2020, p. 4).

It is the Lord Jesus Christ, our Savior and Redeemer, who personally invites each of us as members of His restored church, to help Him know the joy of gathering Israel to the restored gospel of Jesus Christ. My wife and I will share numerous experiences from real life about bringing the joy of the sacred gospel to any of God's children who are invited to come into the Church in these last days. We all can do this! You can do this! There is so much joy for all involved in this sacred undertaking as we move ahead in faith to do all we can for the Lord and his purposes.

In the past sixty years we have seen missionary work in the Church characterized by slogans and phrases, and recommendations from our leaders. "Every member a missionary." "Open your mouth." "Lengthen your stride." "Uniform system for teaching investigators." "Preach My Gospel." There were six formal missionary discussions. Now there is flexibility to teach lessons in whatever way best helps people prepare for conversion. Especially in the era of electronic and digital elements of missionary work, we are learning that somehow we must be able to introduce and teach and then bear testimony to God's precious children.

Three words epitomize all of these plans, lessons, methods, procedures, programs, etc.:

FIND, TEACH, BAPTIZE

We will not see missionary success without these fundamental actions in place. The missionary success stories cited in this humble effort to help gather Israel are each a testimony to find, teach, and baptize, and bring the joy of the Lord to our own lives and the lives of those we help convert to this glorious gospel.

Converts come into the Church with countless backgrounds. Having seen, lived by, adapted, learned, taught, and adhered to the doctrines and practices of a former religion with my family, friends, and leaders, I do not wish to demean my former church and religion in this presentation. In fact, I was extremely fortunate in my many years of association with President Gordon B.

Hinckley, Prophet and President of The Church of Jesus Christ of Latter-day Saints, to be invited by him to discuss my conversion experience in coming into this church. He would call me to his office, invite me to sit with him on airplane travel, ask me to join him at meals, and just simply question me about the process of being a convert to the restored gospel from a predominant church of our time. He said the following in 1998, "Let me say that we appreciate the truth in all churches and the good which they do. We say to the people, in effect, you bring with you all the good that you have, and then let us see if we can add to it. That is the spirit of this work" (*Ensign,* August 1998).

Just a few weeks ago President Russell M Nelson spoke to the Saints in California and admonished them to "figure out ways that our missionaries could find, teach, and baptize using the internet", and in referring to missionaries in all missions to "continue to use all of the wonderful tools to find, teach, and baptize using smartphones." (Church News, Week of March 5, 2022)

This book testifies of these divine principles of missionary work for all of us, members and missionaries, with over six dozen examples of find, teach, and baptize during our family's years in the Church! In addition, in the recent 2022 April General Conference of the Church, we were taught the following doctrines of sharing the Gospel with others: "each of us has a role to play in the gathering of Israel," "find those who are ready to learn about the Restoration of the gospel of Jesus Christ," "press on in the work of the Lord," "our humble desire is for the Savior's teachings to be honored by all," "maintain the mighty change by ministering and missionary work," and "come to Christ for peace in this life."

I sincerely wish to follow that counsel. I have divided this book into 12 chapters, each one describing a different way that you can assist in this great latter-day work of gathering Israel. I desire to share my testimony, and the testimonies of dozens of others, about the glorious joy of being invited to join the Lord's Church in these latter days.

1

Jesus Christ is the Center of the Joy of the Gospel

W hile a young man, I walked paths of life that were different from those taught in The Church of Jesus Christ of
Latter-day Saints. I lived by a mingling of the doctrines and commandments of men, having a form of godliness but with a lack
of God-given truths and the power thereof. Religion was a vital
part of my life as a youth. A religious home was at the core of our
family life. Yet something was missing; something fundamental
about the purpose of life was clouded and uncertain. While in my
young adult years I was fortunate enough to become acquainted
with kind Latter-day Saints who opened new gospel doors to me.

The doctrines of the restoration of the gospel of Jesus Christ
have become my path to eternal life and the fulness of joy here in
mortality. Few things in life have become more dear to me than
knowledge of the reality of the Godhead. We are the literal spirit
offspring of God the Father. The life and mission of His Only Begotten Son, Jesus Christ, affects my life daily. The influence of the
Holy Ghost from day to day is a great comfort.

I came into this Church because God has revealed Himself to
latter-day prophets and they have testified of His reality. Upon

asking God if the things of this gospel are true, I have received a witness more powerful than sight, more soul-assuring than words. The sweet witness by the power of the Holy Ghost that the truths of the restored gospel are upon the earth today has come to me. It has been my profound blessing to become a convert to this Church and to know without a doubt of the divinity of Jesus Christ as the Son of God. This resurrected, perfected being stands at the head of this Church. It is He upon whom we must build. It is He who is the chief cornerstone of our foundation. He is the rock of our salvation, the rock upon which not only the Church will be built, but our personal testimonies as well. No man, yea, no other name under heaven will suffice for our foundation. The prophet Helaman spoke of this sacred foundation most powerfully when he said:

"And now, my sons, remember, remember that it is upon the rock of our Redeemer, who is Christ, the Son of God, that ye must build your foundation; that when the devil shall send forth his mighty winds, yea, his shafts in the whirlwind, yea, when all his hail and his mighty storm shall beat upon you, it shall have no power over you to drag you down to the gulf of misery and endless wo, because of the rock upon which ye are built, which is a sure foundation, a foundation whereon if men build they cannot fall" (Helaman 5:12).

Not only must we build upon the sure foundation of Jesus Christ, but the prophet Jacob identified Him as the "safe foundation!" This stone, he said, shall be "the great, and the last, and the only sure foundation" (Jacob 4:15-16).

I agree with all the conviction of my being that Jacob's testimony is true. When the Apostle Peter boldly declared of Jesus, "Thou art the Christ, the Son of the living God," Jesus replied,

"Blessed art thou, Simon Bar-jona: for flesh and blood hath not revealed it unto thee, but my Father which is in heaven" (Matt. 16:16-17).

Christ will be revealed to us through the same process that God used with Peter. Christ is always the rock upon which each of us must build, even the rock of revelation.

Please study carefully the enclosed *"The Living Christ"* document which is a latter-day witness of the true doctrine of Christ (Appendix II).

Is there opposition from the enemy of all righteousness? Of course!

We may think we are serving God when in reality we are caught up in deceptive teachings. Man may think he believes in Christ, when in fact he does not know or follow the true and living Christ. Many people deny him through the rejection of his living prophets, and additional revealed scripture. Furthermore, man may deny Christ by rejecting the only true and living Church of Jesus Christ upon the earth.

Some years ago, a General Authority Seventy taught the following:

"In the premortal world, Lucifer rebelled against God and His plan, and his opposition only grows in intensity. He fights to discourage marriage and the formation of families, and where marriages and families are formed, he does what he can to disrupt them. He attacks everything that is sacred about human sexuality, tearing it from the context of marriage with a seemingly infinite array of immoral thoughts and acts. He seeks to convince men and women that marriage and family priorities can be ignored or abandoned, or at least made subservient to careers, other achievements, and the quest for self-fulfillment and individual autonomy. Certainly the adversary is pleased when parents neglect to teach and train their children to have faith in Christ and be spiritually born again. Brothers and sisters, many things are good, many are important, but only a few are essential" (D. Todd Christofferson, General Conference, *Ensign*, May, 2005).

It is my personal testimony to you that opposition to truth is real. Satan is terribly miserable and seeks that we will also be miserable. Imagine the schemes he offers knowing that the end result is torment and misery. His weeping, and wailings, and gnashing of teeth are forever imprinted upon the minds of those who have thrown off his powers. His viciousness and wrath are indescribable. The chains that encircle him are a very real evidence of the bonds with which he attempts to encircle the children of God. I know Satan opposed me. I know he seeks to oppose all the words and works of God and Christ.

My parents were devout Christian people who were members of the Catholic Church. I was born in Wenatchee, Washington, and lived my youth in Brewster and Bridgeport, small farming communities bordering the Columbia River north of Wenatchee. Forty-four days after my birth I was baptized in the usual manner under the care of the local parish priest. My baptism was witnessed by my parents along with an uncle who was invited to be my godfather and my grandmother who was an ever-watchful godmother. My middle name, Jerome, was from Saint Jerome, a patron saint in the Catholic tradition of monks and scholars. To my knowledge, this religion was a strongly established tradition in my paternal ancestry for many generations.

For the next twenty-one years I was reared and instructed under the influence of my family's adherence to these religious teachings. My parents raised their five children, I being the eldest, in what they understood to be righteous paths. I am indebted to them for the training and care I received under their guidance. If it had not been as sound as it was, perhaps I would never have cared about seeking the true gospel of Jesus Christ.

At age ten I was confirmed a member of the church in a special ceremony conducted by the bishop of the Yakima, Washington diocese who came to our little town. This was a significant event in the lives of many of us throughout the region. It was on this occasion that the bishop said to me privately, "Gary, someday you will become a priest. In fact, someday you will become a bishop." Quite a statement! I became a priest at age 21 in The Church of Jesus Christ of Latter-day Saints in 1963 and a bishop in 1980 at the age of 39! I had a lot of pre-training for this latter-day service.

What can we do for others who "because of the traditions of their fathers" (Mosiah 1:5) are content to live their lives without the benefit of the restoration of the doctrines of Christ for salvation and eternal life? The answer: Teach the truth. Our Father in Heaven loves all of His children. We are all enabled to return to

His presence through the ordinances of salvation administered by true servants of Jesus Christ. This process is called conversion to The Church of Jesus Christ of Latter-day Saints. It is this process of bringing people to the restored gospel of Jesus Christ that we are going to explore as we seek the joy of the Gospel.

I am one who has been converted to the marvelous events of the Restoration, and most of all to the true teachings of our Lord and Savior. I have been taught in the ways of the prophets and apostles of the latter days. This has brought me out of the limited light of my fathers and into the joyous and beautiful and fulfilling light of the Restoration. This enlightenment is possible for all of our friends who have an interest in the Church. Note how these principles of sharing the truths of the gospel wherever we are will bring forth the joy the Lord has taught us to seek.

Elder C. (Costa Rica San Jose East Mission; reassigned to Maryland Baltimore Mission, 2019-2021):

"To say the least, I have had an interesting mission. I started my mission experience in July of 2019 within the walls of the CCM (Centro de Capacitación Missional) in Mexico City, Mexico. After an amazing six weeks of learning and experiences, I flew to Costa Rica to start my mission assignment. I was very blessed to spend nearly eight months in the wonderful country of Costa Rica. I had three areas, four companions, and many many stories. However, as we know, the sweeping pandemic of COVID-19 cut my time short in Costa Rica. I was sent home to await further instruction and eventually released as a missionary for a short time. It was a very odd experience because I had gotten sent home, while m twin brother was still in his mission in Ventura, California! I ended up spending a little over two months at home as a released missionary. As released missionaries who hadn't completed their full assignment, we were given two options and asked to pick one by April 30th. The first option was to wait a year and then go back into the mission field with hopes that your original mission would be open. The second option was to serve in a temporary reassignment until your original mission opened or you finished your mission. After thoughtful prayer and inspiration from the April General Conference, I felt like I needed to go back out into the mission field. I waited for my reassignment and was asked to labor in the Maryland Baltimore Mission, reporting June 3, 2020. In the Maryland Baltimore Mission, I have served in 3 missions: my first, in York, Pennsylvania Spanish Speaking; my second in Baltimore, Maryland Spanish Speaking; my third, in Columbia, Maryland Spanish Speaking. I am currently serving in the Columbia area with about 19 months in the mission.

"I would like to share an experience from my mission that has really has an impact on me. I was in my first area in Costa Rica called Puerto Viejo de Sarapiqui. We were tracting in this little town called Naranjal one day. This town was a 30-minute walk from Puerto Viejo and it was a secluded town in the jungle near a large river and a banana plantation. It was a very poor and very small town with gravel roads and small houses with tin roofs. We were walking along a road and we came upon a house filled with people on the front porch. It was intimidating because we were strangers passing by and they were all staring at us. I had the impression that I needed to swallow my embarrassment and talk to them. I approached them and started talking. I don't really remember exactly what was said but I remember feeling a sense of relief after the little talk. We were told that we could come by later that week. *FIND* We came by later that week and talked to the father of the large family. His name was Geovany. He was an older man that came out of the house with no shirt. He was very nice and we talked a little bit. When we first started teaching him, though, I believe he listened to us out of kindness and not necessarily out of interest. *TEACH* However, after many lessons, he became a little more interested and open to hear us. We taught him quite a few lessons and invited him to church but there was always something that came up that prohibited him from going. The transfer day came shortly after and I was transferred to my second area of the mission. However, one of my MTC friends was going to my first area! I was excited for him to meet all the people I had taught. Time went by and about a month later, my MTC friend sent me an email with some big news. Geovany had come to church the week after I left, and he loved it! He became eager to hear the missionaries and go to church. He received all the lessons, and attended church, BAPTIZE and got baptized a few weeks after I left. After his baptism, he received the priesthood and blessed the sacrament the following week. A few weeks after that he was called to be Elders Quorum president! I was ecstatic to hear the news! I never thought that my simple action of talking with him months beforehand would lead to such a profound result. I was amazed and I thanked Heavenly Father for allowing me to be part of Geovany's conversion. It was a very special experience that completely changed my perspective of the mission. I remember thinking that a miracle like that always starts with one little act. I'm grateful that I followed the Spirit's prompting that day. If I hadn't, I would've never experienced the joy of seeing one of God's lost sheep come back into the fold. It was a very dear experience that I will never forget."

However, in order for more of us to accomplish this task, we must understand the spiritual foundation our friends and neighbors already have. Then, as our circle of love and concern for prospective members widens and we help them overcome the traditions that may hold them back from the truth, baptisms will surely follow. The day will come when we will sit at the water's edge with one of our friends or receive a cherished letter from those we fellowshipped and in it will be penned the words, "Thank you for helping me find this joy." We long for the day when we will have the thrill of answering that great question, "What must I do to become a member of your church?" If we focus our attitude upon understanding the overall spiritual development of the prospective member, as well as sharing the truth, we will succeed, and we will see the Lord help us accomplish the "thing which he commandeth" (1 Nephi 3:7). This was the case with a family in Duarte, California.

I was serving as the mission president of the California Arcadia Mission. FIND It was a late-night appointment, but the missionaries insisted that a family In Duarte, California, wanted to ask me questions about my conversion. The F. family asked how I felt

7

about leaving my former church because they, too, were making a great change in their lives to leave their church. *TEACH* It was a beautiful hour together, and they were assured that their struggle was known of God and that He would help them make the correct decisions. My heart filled to overflowing at this opportunity. I testified of my profound gratitude for the Book of Mormon, the key to my conversion. I shared my feelings of abandonment from having left my former faith. I could truly feel their concerns over breaking away from family ties and traditions, and over the kind of commitment their decision would require. *BAPTIZE* This family of four was baptized shortly after that visit. They had been shown the truth and were committed to overcoming the barriers that often come with deciding to be baptized. In order to remain anchored in the gospel, they were given support in their efforts to make such a major change in their lives. The whole ward, led by their special friends stepped forward and took this family into their hearts. Many opportunities to serve others were opened to them. The father of this family has served as the bishop in the same ward they lived in when they were baptized. Their spiritual foundations served as a stepping stone as they sought the truth.

I believe that the Lord will help us become more personally involved in understanding and appreciating the previous religious experiences of prospective members as we help them fully come unto Christ. Members can become agents of the Lord in bringing about His purposes. I know we can assist others in these matters and they can know the joy of the Lord.

FIND A man from Russia who had been in the Armenian Orthodox Church for more than ten years was found by our missionaries in California and overcame the traditions of his fathers that had extended for many generations. We met with him on several occasions, and our friendship grew as brothers in the sharing of our conversion struggles. He resonated warmly to principles of the Restoration, in particular priesthood authority and latter-day revelation. *TEACH* As missionaries, we shared with him the beautiful, restored truths of the Book of Mormon and discussed how they deepen our understanding of the doctrines of Christ. *BAPTIZE* His baptism was met with elation in the Latter-day Saint community. He called us when he was ordained to the Aaronic Priesthood, again at his Melchizedek Priesthood ordination, and of course when entering the temple for his sacred covenants. I was thrilled with his goal to bring the gospel to others of his former faith. How dearly I regard this man for his courage to accept the restored gospel after being deeply entrenched in previous religious traditions. After faithfully serving in the Church for a few years, Gerald was asked to translate the Book of Mormon into Armenian!

The Book of Mormon teaches that we must ever be on the alert for those precious moments when the true plan of God can be shared. I testify that this work is a labor of joy.

Nephi's counsel to his brothers is appropriate for our friends and associates. We see that our efforts to help them know who they really are in the overall plan of God will be fulfilled. "They ... [shall]come to the knowledge ... of their Redeemer and the very points of his doctrine, that they may know how to come unto him and be saved" (1 Nephi 15:14).

What an awesome responsibility it is for us to bring these precious truths to our brothers and sisters who live beside us and walk the same paths we walk. We can help them build on the traditions of truth that they have been practicing and throw off traditions that keep them from salvation in the kingdom of God. We can help others add upon their righteous beliefs and behaviors as they come to a knowledge of the fullness of the restored gospel. My parents taught me to be religiously minded, and I appreciate and applaud them for their diligent efforts to help us children stay faithful. The spiritual foundation they helped me establish was pivotal in my search for truth. Many converts feel this way about the role of their religious foundations. By building upon the positive aspects of their previous teachings, prospective members can have the strength to take the next steps of further enlightenment, accept the fullness of the gospel, and develop sure foundations that will keep them anchored in Jesus Christ. So many of our Father's children seek this joy.

Elder C. (Mexico Guadalajara/Mazatlán Mission, 1985-1987):

"I was first assigned to Tecoman, Colima, a hot, humid, coastal town. Before leaving the mission office, a missionary asked me 'Que pecado hizo?' or, as someone translated for me, 'What sin have you committed?' With that send off, I was on my way. I traveled for hours by a bus full of people and chickens, unsure of my destination at every stop. Finally we arrived, but as I disembarked my next problem was not knowing where to go next. No one was waiting for me, and I couldn't explain my situation to anyone. After a while a man with a wooden leg approached me and signaled for me to follow him. I figured it was some kind of trick but had no better plan so I followed him through town. He got me to the church and I threw my bags, then myself, over the gated fence. I never saw that man again.

"My companions showed up after what seemed too long, and the work began—except there was no work. No one was being taught. We spent our days following up and knocking doors. I had no language skills. I wanted to participate but couldn't. It was so frustrating. Luckily I didn't know going home was an option and didn't know how I would get there anyway. At one point my only motivation was observing other missionaries that I thought were the biggest wimps around and I thought—if they can do it, I can do it.

"We caught a break a month into things. *FIND* We knocked the door of a family with eight daughters and no sons. They welcomed us in and we were in business. *TEACH* We broke out the only effective teaching tool in our toolbox which was a film strip projector. How long the prohibitively- expensive bulb would last we never knew but we started showing films. Kids came from everywhere to watch. The neighborhood buzzed with excitement and it was standing room only for some of those discussions. For some reason kids found my inability to communicate a novelty and they greeted my arrivals chanting CO-LE-MAN in the streets. All I could do was smile and play with them. I had no idea how effective genuine interest in others could be.

"The husband positioned himself just around the corner in the kitchen and listened in, but never said anything during the lessons. BAPTIZE A few weeks later the family was baptized and we led the mission in baptisms. That's what eight kids can do! They came to every Church activity held, and my understanding is later the father was also baptized. As for the neighborhood kids, local Catholic leadership put an end to their interest.

"The next 20+ months were filled with amazing experiences and challenges. The highest highs and lowest lows, but teaching the B. family and everyone else in the neighborhood was one of my best experiences as a missionary."

2

Growing in Faith

When I was in my early teens I participated faithfully in my religious duties. We were strict adherents to the daily practice of "saying the rosary" before retiring to bed each evening. We would kneel on the wooden floor of the living room and recite the memorized prayers in unison, passing our fingers along the rosary beads from one prayer to another. This recital usually took twenty to twenty-five minutes and seemed incredibly long on some nights after a full day of work or school activities. However, we lived by the motto "A family that prays together, stays together." The rosary was our manner of regular family prayer. This was a religious discipline that kept us humble and prayerful before the Lord. It was also a common practice for me to recite these rote prayers, including the Lord's Prayer from the New Testament, as deemed necessary during our private moments of worship.

This awakening to right and wrong manifested itself in another way also. In my maturing there began to be the need to resolve serious religious issues in my mind. Some of my friends had entered the seminary for training in religious vocations. I was sharing my faith with others, and they were being led to join in my religious beliefs. But I was troubled by the fact that priests could not marry. I reasoned that if marriage was ordained of God, and I believed it was, how could it be wrong to be married if a man was ordained to the priesthood? Somewhere deep in my being I felt it was right to raise an honorable family. That idea seemed to haunt me each time I pondered going to the seminary to become a priest. Some of the other doctrines of my faith did not seem to square with my scripture study. I was confused about the Trinity and the definition of God and Jesus and the Holy Spirit, yet I did not challenge the authority of my leaders. I tried to have more faith and belief in the mission of the church. My questions heightened and became more meaningful as I passed through certain experiences in my life. One of our sons had the following experience as he sought to do the work of the Lord on his mission.

Elder C. (Argentina Cordoba Mission, 1987-1989):

"We were living in the city of Cordoba Argentina which was generally a large city heavily influenced by the Catholic church. *FIND* While knocking doors we met the Speranza family who were seeking a better understanding about religion and specifically Jesus Christ. *TEACH* We taught the family a few lessons but once extended family members found out they were investigating The Church of Jesus Christ of Latter-day Saints, the opposition became intense and we were asked not to continue discussing baptism. One Sunday we were sitting in the chapel between sacrament meeting and Sunday School and I was feeling unsettled so we decided to leave and visit some of the families we had been teaching. When we knocked on the door of the Speranza family, Sister Speranza opened the door and with an expression of amazement said, 'We had just finished praying that if this was the true Church of Jesus Christ and this was the path for our family, could Heavenly Father please send an answer.' It was right after this prayer was finished that we knocked on their door to see how they were doing. *BAPTIZE*

"Brother Speranza reached out to me in 2007 to let me know he had been serving as a stake president in Cordoba and sent a beautiful note expressing his gratitude and love of the gospel as well as a thank you for having been a part of their miraculous conversion story."

We may not know of the ways a person has been taught by the Spirit and awakened to the difference between right and wrong.

However, we see the fruits of this teaching when he or she makes the choice to accept the full truth of the gospel. This kind of spiritual awakening to right and wrong occurs in the life of many converts.

Nancy was raised in a devout Methodist family. She became uncomfortable with some issues as a teen and fell away, but from then on she searched for which church she should join. As a young wife she took the lessons of the Catholic Church because her husband was from a strong Italian Catholic family and she wanted to share his religion with him.

At this time, Nancy was also expecting their first daughter. She had felt the spirit of her child with her at times and had strong feelings about the divine origin of a new baby. During a group lesson, she heard of the Catholic doctrine that children are born in sin and cannot be saved except through baptism. She was very disturbed by this idea. She knew that it could not be true. Not only did she feel the sanctity of her unborn child, but she had also lost a sister in infancy years before. Nancy told the group during the lesson that she could not believe this doctrine because she knew that little children were innocent. She told them she would not be returning to the lessons.

Months passed, and when her second daughter was born, Nancy was given further spiritual awakening as she looked at her new baby girl. She said, "Welcome to the world," knowing full well, in her heart, that baby Catherine had come from heaven, but not being able to explain how she knew this. Nancy eventually separated from her first husband, her refusal to join the Catholic Church a factor in the decision. As the religion question still plagued her, she would kneel in prayer with her tiny daughters every night, asking the Lord to help her find the right church for them.

FIND Nancy stayed home from work one day, and two sister missionaries knocked on her door. She saw their sweet faces and wondered if they needed something. They talked with her, gave her a Book of Mormon, and invited her to church. Nancy felt the Spirit that first day at church, and she began taking the discussions.

TEACH During one lesson, the missionaries asked her what she thought happened to us in regard to our birth. Nancy responded from her heart, "I believe we came from heaven. I believe we are here to prove ourselves and to be tested. Then we get to go back there." The missionaries were delighted at her answer, wondering how she already knew these truths. This was the plan of salvation. Nancy knew it because she had been given spiritual promptings about the answers to questions she sought. She didn't necessarily know how she had come to her belief, but when the entire plan of salvation was outlined to her, the truth resonated. It was what she had always felt was true, and now she had found a church that taught it as doctrine. *BAPTIZE* Nancy had been awakened to right and wrong, truth and error, long before she joined the Church. This spiritual foundation led her to seek and eventually embrace the restored gospel.

The Book of Mormon plainly depicts this concept of being able to choose right from wrong: "Men are free according to the flesh; and all things are given them which are expedient unto man. And they are free to choose liberty and eternal life, through the great Mediator of all men, or to choose captivity and death, according to the captivity and power of the devil; for he seeketh that all men might be miserable like unto himself" (2 Nephi 2:27). We are all given this choice upon entering mortality.

Some Church members feel that people who have not been baptized and given the gift of the Holy Ghost are not taught by the Spirit. This is simply not true. The Lord said in 1829, before the Church was organized, "Put your trust in that Spirit which leadeth to do good-yea, to do justly, to walk humbly, to judge righteously; and this is my Spirit" (D&C 11:12). The promptings of the Spirit are what lead a person to accept the truths of the gospel. The Spirit awakens them to the difference between right and wrong, and it is what teaches them answers to questions they did not previously know. Many of our friends and neighbors receive lessons from the Spirit before they ever hear about our church. This is because the Lord loves all of His children and wants them all to know His plan of happiness. We cannot discount the teachings of the Spirit that occur in the lives of others. These teachings are meant to guide, heal, and bring comfort. What a beautiful aid the Spirit is in our lives. How wonderful it is to help prospective members come to the waters of baptism. Soon thereafter they will be given the gift of the Holy Ghost. Then they will better understand the spiritual impressions they have had throughout their lives, and they will feel the joy that comes from the gift of the Holy Ghost as a constant companion. Rejoice in how the Spirit helped our son be in the right place at the right time with his missionary duties.

Elder C. (Spain Madrid Mission, 1995-1998):

"My companion, Elder M., and I asked the mission president for special permission to work a 100-hour week. A typical work week was about 60 hours. This meant that we would need to proselyte on p-day, leaving the apartment at about 7:00 am instead of 10:00 am, stay out until 10:30 pm instead of 9:30 pm, and we did not go home for meal breaks.

"One night we were a block from our apartment at about 10:25 pm, and we saw a woman walking by herself across the street. We did not want to startle her so we called to her from across the street that we were missionaries from The Church of Jesus Christ of Latter-day Saints and asked if it would be okay to introduce ourselves. She said that was fine, so we crossed and said hello.

"*FIND* Maria was a single woman from Mexico, working as a live-in nanny for a family who lived nearby. We had a nice chat and she said she rarely got to leave the home where she lived and worked. She could only go out after the children were asleep, which was usually after 10:00 pm. That night she went out to walk to McDonald's, but while we were talking, she remembered that McDonald's closed at 10:00 pm.

"During our brief conversation, she felt the Holy Ghost as we shared a Christ-centered thought, and she invited us to visit her the next day to share a message. *TEACH* Maria was well educated, intelligent, thoughtful, and faithful. She enjoyed her Catholic faith, but she felt something unique during our lessons. *BAPTIZE* After a few lessons she committed to being baptized, and she was baptized a few weeks later.

"Maria was nervous about getting a calling in the ward, but jumped in. With basically no training, she was a gifted Sunday School instructor and was soon serving in the Relief Society presidency of the Madrid 2nd Ward. It would have been almost impossible for us to cross paths if we had not worked the 100-hour week, and if she had not decided to go to McDonald's even though it was closed."

Many of us feel that the more overt or forward approach I have used in sharing the gospel is just not our style. We see and hear of aggressive contacts people make with prospective members, but we hesitate to incorporate those methods in our own approach. Let's face it, some of us just don't feel we have the personality or the assertiveness to be quite so open with others about the gospel plan. So, what can the faithful and happy members of the Church do to be involved? We need not go through life feeling unfulfilled in this portion of the Lord's work. There are many worthwhile contributions and gifts we can offer to help our associates understand the choice that is available through the gospel.

We can make ourselves available to invite prospective members into our homes or take them to Church activities or meetings and be wonderful member missionaries. Can't we merely visit people in their front yard, at the store, while watching a ball game, or while out for a walk and feel we are doing missionary work? Of course we can. Many gospel themes can be brought into our everyday conversations. Consider these simple things that can involve each of us in helping others feel an awakening to the truths of God. Activities like these will help us overcome personal fears about the conversion process and help us fellowship our friends and neighbors. Our local missionaries of the Utah Layton Mission shared this experience:

Elder D. and Elder A. (Utah Layton Mission, February 2021):

"A family we know well had been talking with us for a while about how they want to be better at sharing their testimony of

Christ. One day, they had someone working at their house, and they asked about his belief in God. He responded that he had always thought about joining our Church. *FIND* They happily put him in contact with us!

TEACH "In the first lesson, we began to teach about the restoration of Christ's church, and the member there bore powerful testimony of how God has more He wants to give us. This man replied that he knows God has more to give us and he wants to receive it.

"We were blessed to teach this man a couple of times before introducing him to the missionaries who serve in his area. Though we weren't directly involved, we were excited to hear as he continued learning and faithfully overcame the challenges that surfaced. *BAPTIZE* Then, just over a month after we first met him, we got to attend his baptism over video call.

We know that the Lord is turning this pandemic to the benefit of His work. We are learning better how to encourage members of Christ's church in their missionary efforts, and we love sharing the joy of bringing people to Christ with them!"

Woven into the Book of Mormon are accounts of people to whom the Lord's love was dearly manifest through caring associates who blessed their lives by sharing the gospel with them, giving them the choice to come unto Christ. Such a case is the moving account of the rebellious Zeezrom, who was brought to a change of heart and repentance of his anti-Christ attitude through the power of the gospel. Though sick with a burning fever and the tribulations of his errant ways, he "began to take courage" (Alma 15:4) as he was prompted to seek the teachers of the gospel of Jesus Christ. He afterward joined the ranks of the faithful missionaries and preached the simple, saving doctrines of the word of God (Alma 31:6). What a choice he made between right and wrong! He was certainly awakened to the knowledge of the gospel and chose to live a life of righteousness.

We can all pray that the doors of people in our wards or branches will be opened to the gospel, that hearts will be softened, prepared, and changed. *Pray* for the missionaries to have success and to be guided to the honest in heart. *Pray* for guidance in selecting a family to work with; then select one and begin making special fellowshipping contacts with them. May I illustrate the powerful awakening to God's plan that occurred in my doctor friend whose wife was a new member of the Church.

My wife, Judith, and I became acquainted with this couple through activities and socials with members. FIND Early in April, a stake president and I visited their home at the request of the man's wife, who said she had been praying for someone to help her husband. The doctor chose to honor his wife's desire to have him learn more about the gospel. He was very open to our discussion. He made arrangements for the missionaries to visit three times in the following week. His decision to learn about the gospel was most welcome.

TEACH He invited the missionaries to visit their home many times and opened his heart to the opportunities the gospel offers. BAPTIZE The doctor then asked us to participate in his baptism in mid-April. The following week he was ordained, received a calling in the stake with his wife, and moved forward beautifully in the gospel. We shall never forget the Lord's hand in helping him with his decision to embrace the truth. Several months after the baptism. the doctor was invited to say a prayer at a special fireside. He responded. "I cannot be at the fireside that evening, President. I am going to be with my wife at our first temple preparation class." This man, who had been educated in higher schools of learning, had now chosen to pursue greater knowledge and blessings available in the temple. The prayers of his wife had been answered. My faith was strengthened by his desire to do what was right for his family and act upon his awakenings to the truth.

Another way we can offer prospective members the opportunity to choose the truth of the gospel is to be more *kind*, more *courteous*, and more *aware* of those who live within the boundaries of our influence. In one ward, members welcome newcomers who move into the ward-members or not-and make them feel at home. This type of fellowshipping creates wonderful attitudes about how to reach out to others and how to be friendly toward new neighbors. It also presents our neighbors with the chance to know the truth of the gospel.

Along with prayer and fellowshipping, we can let the *love of Christ* extend into all our associations. We can watch for opportunities to be helpful to the children, the teenagers, the aged, the sick, the shut-in, and the mothers and fathers who are our neighbors. We can visit the sick, visit with young couples, give attention to toddlers, and share flowers or garden produce with neighbors we are acquainted with on our block. This member missionary principle is shown in the example of a Church member named Karen. *FIND* Imagine the surprise of Karen's new neighbor, Catherine, as Karen ran by her home in her jogging suit and left her a small gift and a special greeting! Catherine was deeply touched. *TEACH* As subsequent visits continued to produce the same warm feeling inside, she recognized the truth of the gospel and made the choice to be baptized. *BAPTIZE* What joy followed this courageous choice!

What else can we do to develop long-lasting relationships with neighbors? We should strive to be more *tolerant* of the beliefs, customs, and habits of others. Through this attitude we will be more accepting and more willing to share, to listen, and to demonstrate our faith. Understanding and tolerance will move us further along the road of missionary work than any other attitude. It is a Christlike love that touches the hearts of our friends and neighbors. We must be more tolerant and understanding.

Also, on Fast Sunday we can, among other things, specifically *fast* for the gospel to be taken to people in our area and for the Lord to raise up a family to introduce to the gospel. A young couple sought the Lord's help in this manner. Within a year, another couple of their acquaintance announced that they had made the choice to join the Church.

Along with fasting, we should strive to *live the gospel* and *keep the commandments* so that the Spirit of the Lord will be manifest among us as Latter-day Saints and thus influence our neighbors to be attracted to us. One family had heard that members of our church weren't Christians, but from their own experience they came to the opposite conclusion and sought out the missionaries. This family had clearly been taught right from wrong. They actively sought to make correct choices and were led to the truth of the gospel through the actions of their neighbors.

These simple ideas will help us break down our barriers of fear and increase our participation in meaningful efforts to bring about conversion. Simple, everyday experiences will lend support to helping others find the truth. Through following suggestions such as these, no Church members need to feel that they cannot be helpful in awakening others to right and wrong and to directing them to conversion. My conversion was preceded by an understanding of making choices and being accountable for my decisions. Many prospective members have been similarly taught by the Spirit and have a religious foundation. These awakenings to truth can lead our neighbors to make the ultimate choice to accept the gospel of Jesus Christ. I encourage you to be the means by which this awakening to further light and knowledge occurs, thus finding the joy that comes from bringing the gospel to others. This is true ministering to the children of our Heavenly Father.

3

Seeking Truth

O ne of my high school classmates was a member of The
Church of Jesus Christ of Latter-day Saints. I knew nothing
of his religion, nor did I ever ask him about it. He did impress me
as a person who knew what he wanted out of life, but I did not
relate that to his religious beliefs. I should have, but I couldn't,
because in my church it was a grievous or mortal sin to look at or
become involved with another religion. Neither he nor I knew, at
that time, that he was opening a missionary door just a crack to
me. Not being able to freely discuss other religions created a huge
dilemma for anyone who had doubts or questions about finding
new truths. I did not know that the Lord had said decades before
to a latter-day prophet, "There are many yet on the earth among all
sects, parties, and denominations, who are blinded by the subtle
craftiness of men, whereby they lie in wait to deceive, and who are
only kept from the truth because they know not where to find it"
(D&C 123: 12). It was truly a circumstance of "be wrong if you do
and be wrong if you don't." It was this very dilemma that plagued
me every step along the way of my entry into the world of the
restored gospel.

In the fall of 1959 I left home for Washington State University
in Pullman. I immediately became a member of the Catholic Youth
Organization and continued to regularly attend church and serve
mass in the local community parish. However, I brought my concerns about becoming a priest with me. Was now the time to enter

the seminary? An education in the seminary would have provided college-level training. The curriculum would have brought a religious vocation for the rest of my life. Concerns plagued me. The doctrine of celibacy was the most serious barrier. It just did not seem right to live that way. Though entering the seminary would have been viewed as totally honorable and appropriate in my family and among peers, I could not gain any measure of peace about this career path.

One of the most troubling questions I had about Catholic doctrine was that of the Godhead. This is a common concern for many prospective members and friends. They want to understand God and Jesus Christ. The Book of Mormon prophets taught the simple truths of the Son of God, answering the questions that so many of our friends and neighbors have about the Savior.

"And he shall be called Jesus Christ, the Son of God, the Father of heaven and earth, the Creator of all things from the beginning; and his mother shall be called Mary" (Mosiah 3:8). The Book of Mormon then goes on to teach about the relationship we have with the Savior when we come to accept the truths found in the gospel: "And now, because of the covenant which ye have made ye shall be called the children of Christ, his sons, and his daughters; for behold, this day he hath spiritually begotten you; for ye say that your hearts are changed through faith on his name; therefore, ye are born of him and have become his sons and his daughters" (Mosiah 5:7). During my high school and early college years, I needed these answers. I searched for these truths just as many of our friends and loved ones search for them.

Sister C. (Brazil Porto Alegre Mission, 2021-2013):

"I love Porto Alegre! Much more clean than Sao Paulo and so much fun. There are lots of stores..lots…of shopping…and shoes… sorry dad…lol. The people here are great. First off, I love my trainer and couldn't have hoped for better. She is a pretty Brazilian who is a convert and is 24 years old. She is studying to be a lawyer so she is way sharp and has such amazing teaching techniques. *FIND* My president pulled me aside and said she is the best in the mission and to learn from her. I am learning like crazy it is great. I just want to be fluent now but know it will take some more patience! *TEACH* This week in the first lesson we taught she had me invite a 13-year-old girl, Sheila, to baptism. I did and bore my testimony of God's love for her and she agreed to be baptized!! *BAPTIZE* It will be this Sunday! I was so happy and so excited for her I can't describe it. Here you are walking around in heat and dirt and sometimes unbelievably poor houses and yet smiling like crazy and loving life. We are in a nice city but some parts are very very very poor. It is humbling. But you love all the people just the same. We also taught a Catholic family about the restoration and I hope so much to see them baptized!!! We will work so so so hard: at night you are just exhausted but it is good. This week I had the flu so had to rest Saturday and Sunday but am feeling much better now. Today is pouring rain! I like it though. Okay, my thoughts are so scattered so much is going on that I want to say but just know that I am so happy, feel so perfectly great and truly feel like my life is on the perfect track, and I will try to be more organized next email.

"Yesterday was stake conference and there was a broadcast with the Stevensons and Stanley G. Ellis and Richard G. Scott! At first I was a little overwhelmed because I don't understand everything and felt lost haha. However, Stanley G. Ellis got up and gave his talk in Portuguese! It was so cool. And then Richard G. Scott got up and spoke in Portuguese as well! It was incredible. I didn't know they spoke this language and wish I could describe the comfort that I felt hearing Richard G. Scott who I love speak in Portuguese. I think they were in Sao Paulo. I just really felt connected and that Heavenly Father hears and answers prayers. I hope everyone is doing wonderful and love you much!"

Consider how sharing a copy of the Book of Mormon with someone will help them learn about Jesus Christ. Write your brief testimony about the book in the front of the book. A person must be given the opportunity to read the Book of Mormon in order to sup from its pages and find answers to questions they seek. Such was the case with the following woman.

FIND She came to my office with a member who was a leader in our church and was seeking counsel about how a Catholic woman could resolve some personal concerns. The counselor had told her of my Catholic background and suggested she visit with me about the matter. Our conversation concluded, and then I recommended she consider and pray about a more long-range solution to her needs. She accepted a Book of Mormon and promised to meet with me later. Days passed, and then she called to visit with me again. Upon her arrival, she said, "I came to see if you could help me learn about the Church." *TEACH* I arranged for the missionaries immediately. She was taught and prepared for baptism in three weeks. Radiant and full of joy, she eagerly sought to enter the kingdom of God. The night of her baptism I called the Castleton family in Ogden, Utah. *BAPTIZE* As she entered the church for the baptismal service, I asked her to speak to Sister Castleton on the phone. Sister Castleton asked, "How are you, and what are you doing at the church today?" Our friend replied in a way that brought unspeakable joy to those of us involved. She said she had read the Book of Mormon that the Castleton family had donated to her through the mission and that she was at the church to be baptized! The truths in the Book of Mormon had led her to the waters of baptism, and the Castleton family's faithfulness in this effort helped make the distribution of this sacred book possible. It was a simple act of ministering with a life-changing effect.

Our friends and neighbors need to be given the opportunity to find the answers they seek, and we can be a factor in bringing this about. Members of the Church have been termed the "sleeping giant" of missionary efforts. Should this sleeping giant, the more than sixteen million members of the Church, awaken to its full potential, literally millions of people could join the Church every year. As we develop the faith and courage to assist others in the search for truth, we can experience the growth that President Nelson envisions today. We can reach new spiritual heights. We can partake of the joy that comes as we heed the Lord's counsel concerning missionary work. What a beautiful story is shared here by one family member serving in Portugal:

Sister J. (Portugal Lisbon/Porto Mission, 2014-2016):

"I was transferred to Viseu in the end of April of 2015. I was opening an area that had been closed and was training a new missionary all at the same time. In early May we had an interview with our mission president. At this interview he extended me a challenge to baptize in the month of May. He asked if I would accept and not wanting to refuse a challenge from my mission president I said yes. However, in my mind I thought, "This is never going to happen. We have been in this area for maybe 5 days and have no investigators other than a young man with whom we had a heated discussion about religion the day before in the street, but still agreed to speak with us again.

"As I left the interview I had the sickest feeling in my stomach. As we walked home I just felt worse and worse. I knew I needed to repent and to have more faith that my mission president would not have extended an invitation like this lightly. I remember praying so hard that night for forgiveness and that we would be led to those prepared in the area.

"*FIND* We continued to meet with the young man from the street. His name was Andre, and he had strange beliefs in what's called spiritualism. As we continued to work hard to find others, it seemed like every day Andre was becoming more receptive to the gospel. He was reading from the Book of Mormon daily and praying about what we taught him. *TEACH* We asked him if he wanted to be baptized and he told us maybe in a year or so. As the month was coming to a close I one day had the strongest impression to ask him again to be baptized. Sitting in front of the church on the steps after church we asked Andre again if he would be baptized. We asked for a date in June towards the end of the transfer, knowing that it was not in the month we had been challenged to baptize in. *BAPTIZE* To our surprise, he said that he had a dream the night before of his grandma letting him know that what he was doing was right. He said he wanted to honor her and to be baptized in May on the anniversary of her death.

"To me this was the biggest testimony of my mission that the Lord does have people prepared. We just need to have faith, get out of our own way, and allow Him to lead us to those who are ready. Andre has since been to the temple and served a mini mission in Spain and continues to serve faithfully in the Church."

4

Always More to Learn

My university years were filled with new experiences, friends, and preparation for my future. I think I changed my major and selection of a particular degree to pursue at least four times in those years. I wandered from agricultural engineering to political science to vocational education, finally settling on physical education and psychology in the ranks of professional teaching. During my early college days, my father had become hospitalized, my mother was having a tough time caring for the family, and it was difficult to stay focused on my future. I was tempted to return home and abandon my college pursuit. My financial situation was bleak as well, and I was living from day to day on student jobs at night to supplement my summer income, taking out a student loan each fall to cover tuition and housing expenses. I paid the loans back each summer but sought a new loan faithfully each fall. It was a very uncertain time in my life. For three summers I worked for the U.S. Forest Service and learned important lessons about following the counsel of leaders.

I have drawn upon my experience in the Forest Service time and time again as I found my way into the plan of God through the restored gospel. Years ago I heard a phrase that would guide me all my Church life. "Follow the Brethren," my home teaching companion would counsel as we visited our assigned homes. "Keep your eye on the prophet" was a favorite saying of this mentor in the gospel. I have learned many applications of that experience as I have trusted the servants of the Lord. We can pick out reference points in life to help us work toward our goal. Though we may carry heavy packs in life, the prophets will help us keep ourselves properly oriented, and we will not get lost and discouraged and fail to reach our goal of helping others in their search for the gospel. Though we may tread new ground and the fear of the unknown may seem to close about us even as the tall trees deep in the forest, we can put our trust in such reference points as the prophets, the scriptures, and the programs of the Lord. As we note the clearings and open places along our journey, we can catch our breath and strengthen our resolve to reach our goal. Our grandson explored new routes and places seeking to help a person for whom very little was known.

Elder L. (Taiwan Taipei Mission, 2015-2016):

FIND "On a Monday morning in December, my companion and I checked the newly-launched Global Referral system. There was a message that read, 'There was a foreign exchange student here in Mesa, Arizona. Her name is Ariel. Here is her address. She has a Book of Mormon.' Okay, what? That is not much to go off. We had no idea where this place was.

"We found ourselves at the end of a 45-minute bike ride standing in front of a 19-story apartment building with the entry door locked. We rang a few doorbells, and someone eventually let us in the building. This exchange student lived on the 19th floor, so up we went, to the top. Her door was on the right. We stepped up and knocked. The door opened and in front of us was a very small, adorable Taiwanese lady in her mid-40's who about jumped out of her skin when she saw us. We asked if Ariel was home and explained her American friends had sent us. Luckily, she knew her daughter's English name. Turned out she was home but in the shower, so we asked if we could come back in 20 minutes. With a hesitant yes from the mother, we left.

"We came back and met Ariel, a 17-year-old Taiwanese girl who had lived with an LDS family in Mesa, Arizona for a year as an exchange student. *TEACH* She was surprised to see us but interested to hear more about this religion her host family had shared a bit with her, especially in Chinese. We taught her a couple of times a week for a few weeks. After a bit, her mother, Jiang Ma (as we lovingly called her meaning "Mama Jiang") started to join us as well. After only a couple of weeks, we asked Ariel if she wanted to be baptized. BAPTIZE She said yes, but that she always envisioned herself being baptized on her birthday if she was baptized because it was her rebirth. We asked her when her birthday was, it was January 19th, only two weeks away. We let her know that if she wanted, she could be baptized on that birthday. Ariel was so excited at the idea and said yes immediately.

"Two weeks later Ariel was baptized on her birthday. There was a nice turn out from the ward, especially some youth who had joined us at some of our lessons. Ariel was excited and felt very happy about the experience. I love these two sisters and it is a joy to keep in touch with them."

Just as the forest smoke is a constant beacon, sometimes seen but more often not seen, so also are the prophets and the gospel a constant aid and comfort in our journey through life. The Lord has given us prophets to guide us and beckon us to better ourselves and others along the way. Living the gospel will help us stay on ridgelines, where our vision is not cluttered and our ability to share the gospel is enhanced. The Prophets always counsel us to share the gospel with others.

The best support system for our full-time missionaries is strong member involvement in the conversion process. Elder Dallin H. Oaks, a member of the Quorum of the Twelve, has said that until members become more effective in sharing the gospel, "these wonderful full-time missionaries—our sons and daughters and our noble associates in the Lord's work—will remain underused in their great assignment to teach the restored gospel of Jesus Christ" ("Sharing the Gospel," *Ensign*, November 2001, pg.7). Stake and ward councils must help members capture the great potential of these full-time servants of the Lord. Missionary efforts can be correlated regularly through appropriate meetings and opportunities to counsel together about individual needs of investigators and converts. All of us are working to build up the Church as the prophet Alma taught: "And they were called the church of God, or the church of Christ, from that time forward. And it came to pass that whosoever was baptized by the power and authority of God was added to his church" (Mosiah 18:17). A great deal of our efforts in today's world are involving media, virtual contacting, and texting correspondence. But the personal element of talking to people will always be needed.

Let me cite an example of an occasion when my wife and I followed the counsel of the prophets to find a "referral of great promise." Our family moved into a new home after months of seeking the situation best suited for our needs. FIND One Sunday afternoon following our relocation, my wife, Judith, and I spent a few hours becoming acquainted with our neighbors. We met two families by introducing ourselves to them and briefly telling them about our family. It was a good experience, and we felt accepted by these neighbors. It was also interesting that as we mentioned to our neighbors that we were members of The Church of Jesus Christ of Latter-day Saints, they responded, "Yes, we know!" Somehow our Church identity preceded us.

One of the families we met was a young couple with four children close to the ages of our children. Gary and Phyllis were soon to become our very close friends. Just a few days after we met this family, my wife was visiting with Phyllis in their front yard. This was the beginning of a very open relationship. Judith and Phyllis became good friends and shared a great deal of time with each other. It was comfortable for these two women to be in each other's homes. Gary and I also began to share more time together. Soon their family joined our family at church for various family activities.

TEACH I asked Gary if he would like his family to learn more about our church and to have our missionaries meet with them. We told Phyllis and Gary that we would attend missionary discussions with them if they wanted us to. Gary agreed to have the missionaries, and I set an appointment for the elders to teach them.

Following the first discussion, I drove the missionaries home. Upon returning to Gary's home to get Judith, he asked if he could talk to me a moment about his family. He then said he would like to start the new year off right. He asked if it would be possible for me to baptize them on New Year's Eve.

BAPTIZE That was a wonderful moment. Our new friends had already decided to join the Church! We were thrilled for them and thrilled about our missionary efforts in their behalf. Two months later this family was transferred to another city. What if we hadn't met this fine couple and fellowshipped them during the brief period of time when we lived near each other? This father has served as a stake president, a bishop, a mission president with his wife, and a temple president with his wife at his side! The children in the family have served missions. What a return on our investment of time on that Sunday afternoon! How vital was that one referral in the missionary effort!

From that experience and the counsel of latter-day apostles and prophets, we had learned that there are great blessings from the Lord when we work with families to teach the gospel. In recent years our inspired leaders have focused on ways to hold successful family missionary meetings. Here are numerous suggestions for your consideration in sharing the gospel:

- Prayerfully select a family.
- Get acquainted.
- Invite them to your home.
- Inform them that you are Latter-day Saints.
- Invite them to a family home evening.
- Share a copy of the Book of Mormon that includes your testimony.
- Share your feelings about a specific principle or doctrine.
- Ask questions to enhance their interest.
- Ask the missionaries to teach them in your home.

We follow the prophets when we use prayer as a fundamental aspect of sharing the gospel with our neighbors and friends. Members have been asked to prayerfully select a family to friendship into the Church each year. A few years ago I joined with the stake priesthood leaders and missionaries to make missionary home visits. The bishop, a missionary, and I were assigned to visit a family in the ward. We prayerfully sought the Lord's help for this sacred visit. The man's wife had joined the Church many years before. Her Catholic husband had never had the discussions, though he was quite supportive of her Church involvement. *FIND* As we visited with him, there was a sweet spirit of love and acceptance in the room. We prayed again with this kind brother and his wife for strength to be full of faith at this special occasion. We discussed the principles of the gospel and their eternal impact upon him and his wife. *TEACH* At the conclusion I challenged him softly, "Will you hear the discussions from the missionaries?" To my great joy, he accepted the challenge. Over the next three months he worked his way toward baptism. *BAPTIZE* In mid-February, he called and invited me to speak at his baptismal service. What a joyous couple attended the sacred ordinance that Sunday evening! The chapel was filled as friends and Saints all witnessed this glorious event. A seventy-two-year-old man was now beginning a new life with his dear companion. Prayer had been an integral part of the entire missionary process, and the Lord then had a hand in our efforts.

We are capable and loveable messengers and ministers. We have a message to share with our friends and neighbors that can help them find their way through the hazards of the world and come unto Christ. A key element of this message centers on being able to follow living prophets, a new concept to many prospective members. As they come to know the role of Church leaders in guiding them through the thickets of life, they will find great comfort and direction that they had never before known was available. Prophets stand on the watchtowers of life, guiding us to our eternal goals. Let us keep our eye on the living prophets as we take their challenge to spread the gospel and teach others of the blessings that latter-day prophets can ensure.

A business acquaintance called and invited me to have lunch with him. As we discussed various aspects of our pending merger of professional resources, I noted that this man professed high personal ideals. I commented on this during our conversation and his face lit up like a light bulb! He was so pleased to be complimented in that manner. At that point, it was natural and appropriate for me to share my professional and personal standards with him. Immediately our regard for each other was heightened and in just moments I was able to share portions of my religious conviction with him. Upon parting, I gave him a book and asked him to read it as a means of understanding my motivation and philosophy of life. This experience was uplifting and pleasant for me. A missionary door was opened with very little effort on my part. Yet my attitude about being prepared to share the gospel with a colleague was met with success in the first hour of effort.

Elder B. (Uganda Kampala Mission, 2019-2021):

"I was serving in Lesotho as a zone leader in the fall of 2019. Once we were in our area we went about our schedule and went to the appointments we had. I felt a very strong clear impression from the Spirit that there was somebody out there we needed to find at that time and I then told my companion we have somebody we need to find right now. FIND Soon the Spirit said you missed a house so we turned around and went to the one other door. At that door we met a man that was so happy to see us and to learn more about Jesus Christ. TEACH We then started going back and teaching him and his wife. After a few months of teaching them, the brother had gained such a strong testimony of the Savior Jesus Christ, the restored gospel and the Book of Mormon. BAPTIZE This brother was baptized and is still a strong faithful member of the Church. The Spirit clearly guided my companion and I to one of God's elect children who was prepared to receive the gospel."

5

The Joy of Conversion Ahead

In the fall of 1961, my college junior year, I returned to Pullman, Washington, and lived in a second-floor apartment, closer to campus. One evening, several weeks into the fall semester, I met Judith England. She was a member of The Church of Jesus Christ of Latter-day Saints, the first young woman of that faith with whom I had become acquainted. Something unusual happened to me. The moment I saw her, I had what I understood to be a spiritual prompting. As clearly as anything I have ever experienced, I was told she would have a part to play in my future.

In my youth, I had never entertained the thought of joining another church. I felt that I belonged to the true church, and I was not seeking any other way of life. Meeting Judith that night and walking across campus together led us to talk and share ideas and backgrounds. I didn't go for a walk with her to learn about her religion, but her religion was a part of her, just as mine was a part of me. She talked about her goals, innocently and in a straightforward manner. I had never heard of the concepts she was sharing: eternal marriage, celestial kingdom, forever families. But those concepts pricked my heart. It was the doctrine of Christ that was being taught. Though my life had a religious foundation, I could not comprehend the impact these new principles would have upon my life if I were to accept them. They seemed to sink deep into my being, stirring the questions and concerns I had about the sanctity of the family.

My greatest fear was the consequences of challenging the authority and traditional teachings of the church of my youth. Those who have not witnessed this firsthand probably have no idea of the magnitude of such an endeavor. It is not something to be taken lightly or expect will happen easily. It was one of the most difficult decisions I had ever made.

A few weeks later the YMCA sponsored a meeting on campus where an interesting topic was to be discussed. "Mormon Attitude on Life and Death" was the theme, and the presenter was John M. Madsen, a returned missionary who was active in the LDS Institute of Religion on campus. Strange as it seemed, he was also a classmate of mine in a physics course. I had two new friends, both Latter-day Saints, in a period of two to three weeks. What was going on here? John's presentation was in a Student

Union Building lecture room. A nice crowd was present. I know because I paced back and forth in the hallway outside the room for several minutes before I entered. For me to be there was blatant rebellion against my faith. I was choosing to listen to the doctrines of another church, a sin of grave consequences, but what a presentation it was. I learned about the plan of God, our premortal life, mortality, judgment, spirit world, resurrection to differing degrees of glory, and eternal life with God, Jesus, and family. Simplicity, order, and truth stirred my soul. I was feasting upon the word of God in a way I had never known before. Though steeped in the doctrines of my previous church, I had never heard of the Plan of Salvation, the Great Plan of Happiness, the Plan of Redemption, the Great Plan of God! Oh how I was impacted by these true and joyous concepts! I hungered for the truth and answers to my questions. I began to seek out the people and the environment in which I could be taught the things of the Restoration, a new word in my experience. The Latter-day Saints had answers to my questions, all of them. It was a new day, a day of awakening from the traditions of my fathers into a world of truth and light and true joy.

For every question we prayerfully think of to ask, there are dozens of possible answers depending on the varied responses of each individual. Make a concerted effort to understand the beliefs and concerns of your friends without judging them. With a prayer in your heart, you will enjoy peace about the matter. Perhaps we will be asked questions in response to our questions. If so, the door is open for conversation, for sharing. Often the door will open clearly and easily to a special need you can meet. On other occasions, your question will solicit no response or interest at all. Don't be disturbed about that; maybe the person you spoke to just wasn't in the mood to visit. It doesn't take long to get a feeling about pursuing the matter or dropping it. Whatever the case, you have learned more about what feels best for you in these situations. Most of the time you will find that people are willing to talk and visit with you. Just like members missionaries, the prophets of the Book of Mormon were prone to ask questions. Hundreds of questions dot the pages of this great book. Alma the Younger asks forty-two questions in the fifth chapter of Alma, deep and searching questions about life, death, salvation, mercy, prophets, change of heart, faith, and on and on.

Without a doubt, a family we met *FIND* responded to the answers that come from preaching the word. My wife and I met a couple at the baptism of their adult son. Our golden question for them was "Will you be our guests at a regional conference of our Church?" Judith, our son Kent, and I picked up the wonderful family on that beautiful Sunday, and we enjoyed introducing them to local Church leaders in the region. They were deeply touched by the people of The Church of Jesus Christ of Latter-day Saints as a Catholic family. *TEACH* The missionaries and I began to visit and teach them. *BAPTIZE* The mother asked for baptism late that spring after several visits to their home. Her husband said he was going to be next. What a thrill it was to hear of their progress, which had started with a simple question.

Remember, when you ask a golden question, you will be participating in a sacred opportunity to open gospel doors to our Heavenly Father's children. The more you learn from these experiences, the closer you will come to being part of a convert's life. Take a step of faith with a golden question and see where it takes you and your friends. It may be just the question they needed you to ask.

Having served mass as an altar boy for twelve years and having experienced the priest being the center of attraction at a worship service, I was hardly prepared for the scene at the Pullman Ward. Everyone seemed to participate in some way or other. Presiding officials, conducting officials, participating individuals, prayers, music, speakers, youth talks, class teachers, greeters, men leaders, women leaders, and so on. It was overwhelming to me at first. But I shall never forget the friendliness and warmth with which I was received by this group of strangers.

In the fall of 1962, I again returned to WSU. Judith had graduated and was teaching in Spokane, Washington. We were getting more serious about each other, and I was determined to conquer the religion question. John invited me to attend his early morning seminary class for high school students in the Pullman area. I accepted his invitation and became even more engaged in the study of religion. He was teaching a course in Church history, and this introduced me to The Church of Jesus Christ of Latter-day Saints in a truly proper way. Some days I wouldn't attend, but the class would pray me back. My young friends were so encouraging and interested in my questions. They were such a faithful example to me of dedication and commitment to their beliefs. I admired their devotion to the gospel.

Many converts say the reason they investigated the Church was because they knew there was something different about its members. They could feel the love of Christ emanating from those who have come to know Him. They know they are loved by the members of the Church who welcome them into the fold with open arms. Each of us can apply aspects of fellowshipping to our friends and neighbors. All it takes is love and a righteous example.

I know of a doctor's wife who died of cancer, and her member husband said she had been concerned that she had never helped anyone come into the Church. *FIND* This member doctor resolved that her funeral would be a missionary effort in her memory. He knew that many friends in his profession would come to the funeral, including a couple who were both physicians. I agreed to speak for the purpose that this faithful husband outlined. The plan of salvation was taught to his friends and associates on that special day. Only days following the service, the couple contacted our doctor friend, inquired about the doctrinal messages of the funeral, and expressed their desire to learn more about the teachings of the Church. *TEACH* Missionaries were contacted, discussion were presented, my wife and I visited with them and reassured them, and other members rallied to their needs. This sweet experience was repeated as it has been for decades. *BAPTIZE* The sacred ordinance of baptism was performed for two special people who humbled themselves before the Lord in the prescribed manner. Our doctor friend's departed companion had fulfilled her hope after all. The key is to teach the word of God wherever and whenever possible. The prophet Alma has written: "They did go forth, and began to preach the word of God unto the people, entering into their synagogues, and into their houses; yea, and even they did preach the word in their streets" (Alma 32:1).

A frequently mentioned difficulty associated with sharing the gospel is a lack of self-confidence and a fear that people may think we are forcing ourselves upon them. This lack of self-confidence and fear of man translates into interesting concerns about personal involvement in bringing converts to the restored gospel. Many active members of The Church of Jesus Christ of Latter-day Saints feel that their testimony of the gospel is strong, yet they also say they have difficulty sharing the gospel with others. Therefore, Church members often feel that they do their missionary work through one major function: being an example. We can do more.

On Sunday, June 3, 1990, while praying over a particular matter related to a choice family I had been visiting for thirty-five months, I was impressed to invite the father to a special Church program. Leland was a staunch Catholic who honored his wife's Church roots and allowed his children to be raised in and influenced by her church. For twenty years he had accepted assignments in scouting and other Church programs where he could serve his children as they grew in the gospel. *FIND* We first met in the early days of my service as a mission president, and as the months went by, we called each other, visited and even prayed together in his home. All the missionaries assigned to his ward were asked to teach and testify to him month after month. He had friends throughout the community who took an interest in him and his beautiful family. He was included in the activities and projects of the ward and stake family.

Upon arriving home late that morning, I called his wife and assured her that Leland was invited to the program where there would be a special message for him. Much to my delight, he came to the meeting! President James Smith, the stake president, and I challenged him to prepare himself for baptism *TEACH* and set aside the traditions of his fathers that he had been struggling with. In the ensuing two weeks, many people spoke words of faith, love, and testimony to our dear friend. Even as late as Saturday morning, the day before the baptismal service, he had doubts. But after a lengthy home visit, a counselor in the stake presidency received a firm commitment from Leland that he would be baptized. *BAPTIZE* On Father's Day, June 17, in the presence of four former bishops and more than a hundred friends and family members, Leland was baptized. Much rejoicing was witnessed in that stake by all who were present. His son, in the Provo MTC, was notified that his first baptism, though performed by others, was his father. One year later, Leland told me about his sweet experience of attending the temple with his family. Fellowshipping was the key. A continuous outpouring of love over many years softened his heart and led him to the mighty change. How thrilled we are at his continued progress in the gospel as he and his family grow and prosper in callings and service. He was greatly admired for his service as a bishop also!

How are we going to move ahead in this work? As we begin to pray, fellowship, and actively involve ourselves in helping convert others, thousands of families will benefit. Trusting in the word of the Lord and taking steps of faith will help us overcome real barriers of fear and lack of self-confidence. Will you explore ways to fulfill your missionary responsibility and enjoy more involvement in bringing converts unto Christ? We can share ways of taking these steps with each other that will lessen our fears about missionary experiences.

6

The Joy of the Restored Gospel

Later in the fall of 1962, and during my participation in the seminary class, I struggled mightily with the issues of restored religion. In fact, my mind could not be freed from the mental turmoil of joining another church. I was carrying sixteen hours of schoolwork, and it was a real test for me to keep a proper focus on my studies. The truths of the restored gospel of Jesus Christ were beginning to be manifest to me. I had been to a stake conference in Spokane, Washington, where Elder Boyd K. Packer had taught the doctrines of the restored gospel. Though I did not know the truth of these things, I knew that he knew the truth of the things he taught. True conversion was not far away.

FIND John's early morning seminary class was introducing me to the defining doctrines of the restored gospel. I was absorbing the doctrine of Christ through the plain and simple teachings of the Book of Mormon and the events of early Church history. I mention the Book of Mormon here because a copy was given to me just days before my decision to join the Church. I don't know who prepared it for me. (I am referring to the practice, years ago, where members of the Church marked a copy of the Book of Mormon for investigators.) My book had the numbers of various verses circled in red pencil with the words "go to page 30" (for example). The marking system focused on the defining doctrines of the restored gospel. (See Appendix IV.)

TEACH The clear, plain truth about the Godhead-about God the Father, Jesus Christ as His Only Begotten Son, and the Holy Ghost as a testifier and witness of the purposes and plans of the Father and the Son-was clearly illustrated to me. Jesus is the Savior and Redeemer and the only way to salvation and eternal life. Verses were marked referring to the power and authority of God through prophets, apostles, and a holy priesthood. Further, marked verses dealt with principles of faith and repentance and the ordinances of the gospel that lead to eternal life. There was evidence of revelation, inspiration, miracles, and the word of God to man through His appointed servants. There was also the plan. Oh, how I resonated to the plan of salvation, the plan of happiness, the great and eternal plan of God, the plan of mercy, the plan of redemption! The last verses marked in my little blue paperback copy of this testament of Jesus Christ were Moroni 10:3-5, which included these words: "When ye shall receive these things, ... ask God, the Eternal Father, in the name of Christ, *if these things are not true*; and ... he will manifest the truth of it unto you, by the power of the Holy Ghost."

The sequence of events at that point in my life are indelibly etched on my memory, my heart, my mind, and my soul. The following morning, at the seminary class, Brother Madsen introduced us to a recording by President Hugh B. Brown of the Church's First Presidency. I listened carefully and prayerfully. This was a major step for me; letting go of papal and priestly authority was now possible. For months I had learned of Joseph Smith the Prophet. My summer reading had introduced me to him. It was not easy to accept a prophet when I had been taught all my life that a latter-day prophet is a false prophet. The traditions of my church taught that popes and priests represent Christ on the earth and had His authority in a continuous line from the apostles of former days when Christ lived on the earth. In President Brown's "Profile of a Prophet," I still hear, ringing in my ears, his stirring declaration undergirding and overarching all the arguments for or against prophets in the latter-days; Joseph Smith was a prophet of God. I gained a testimony of Joseph Smith the Prophet that very hour. It was a stunning development in my long months of searching for truth. It was such an urgent and overwhelming experience that I could not wait a moment longer to resolve the issue of traditional religion or restored religion. I knew I must resolve the matter of joining the Church or leave it alone once and for all. My studies were suffering since I gave my waking hours to the pondering of religious matters. I had to be so sure in my decision. My example to my family of what religion I chose to live had to be based upon truth, not error. How could I be sure? I resolved to go to the Lord in earnest prayer about my struggle. It was time to do as the prophet Alma had taught when asked by a friend in need of answers: "What shall we do?" The scriptural prompting was, "If ye will awake and arouse your faculties, even to an experiment upon my words, and exercise a particle of faith, yea, even if ye can no more than desire to believe, let this desire work in you, even until ye believe in a manner that ye can give place for a portion of my words" (Alma 32:9, 27).

Immediately I returned to my apartment and poured out my heart to the Lord—not in the rote prayer of my youth but as a son of God seeking answers to questions. I had read the verses in the tenth chapter of Moroni and decided to apply the words of verses 4 and 5. I did ask God, in the name of Jesus Christ, if the precepts I was studying were true. I asked with a sincere heart, with real intent. More than anything I had ever wanted, I wanted to know what to do about religion. I asked about Joseph Smith. I asked about the restoration of the true church. I asked about the Book of Mormon. I asked about the reality of Jesus Christ and His work. I pleaded with the Lord to reveal to me what I should do.

I received the answer to every one of my questions. By the power of the Holy Ghost, from the top of my head to the soles of my feet, I received the answers. I knew the truth of all the things I pondered. I felt a burning in my whole being that removed every doubt, every fear, every concern. Relief and peace came over me. I knew what I must do. Oh, that I could pen the feelings I felt and the knowledge I gained through this manifestation of spiritual power that morning.

I can only declare that I know, by the power of the Holy Ghost, that these things are true. From that time forth, there has never been a doubt. I had never before had such an electrifying experience. I had paid the price to know, in the Lord's way, what to do.

I experienced personally the scriptural promise of the prophet Moroni, the concluding writer in the Book of Mormon. I had asked God in humble and sincere prayer if *these things*, the things I had been pondering for many months, *these things* I had to resolve, *these things* that would take me from false traditions and into the light of the Restoration, were true. Moroni says that God will manifest the truth unto the sincere seeker of *these things*. And God did manifest it. He helped me. He lives. He cares about the son or daughter who asks for help in *these things*. I know, because He cares about me. My faith in Christ was sufficient to merit an answer to my pleadings in the name of Christ. The influence of the Holy Ghost was sent to me about *these things* to allow me to feel that sacred and convincing power in my whole being, undeniably and with full clarity and plainness. I know because I am a witness of the power sent by the Holy Ghost. Was the restored doctrine of the Godhead true? Can there be any doubt as to the reality of *these things* pertaining to the Father, Son, and Holy Ghost? Certainly not to this young man seeking the truth within my small sphere of needs. The Book of Mormon had led me to the plain and precious word of God, and it was having a "more powerful effect" upon my mind than "anything else" that had happened to me. The Book of Mormon, my seminary teacher and class, and latter-day prophets had led me to "try the virtue of the word of God." What power there is in the restored gospel to effect change in the life of a seeker of truth (Alma 31:5). Moroni's promise was fulfilled for me that morning and has been expanded during my years in the Church.

This was the most profound part of my doctrinal conversion. The churches of men had produced great errors in their teachings about the Godhead. Apostasy was rampant on this subject. However, my spiritual experience that morning made clear to me the true doctrine of God. God answered my prayer through the power of the Holy Ghost because I had exercised faith in Christ.

The restored gospel teachings about the Godhead are plain and precious. They were taught when Jesus appeared to the people of the Book of Mormon in the Americas. We read these precious words from God the Father: "Behold my Beloved Son, in whom I am well pleased, in whom I have glorified my name—hear ye him" (3 Nephi 11:7). In response to His Father, the Son replied, "I am Jesus Christ, whom the prophets testified shall come into the world" (3 Nephi 11:10). Could any declaration be clearer than this? Jesus defines His doctrines and the very points of doctrine needed for salvation in His church and kingdom: "Behold, verily, verily, I say unto you, I will declare unto you my doctrine" (3 Nephi 11:31). "Verily, verily, I say unto you, that this is my doctrine, and I bear record of it from the Father; and whoso believeth in me believeth in the Father also; and unto him will the Father bear record of me, for he will visit him with fire and with the Holy Ghost. And thus will the Father bear record of me, and the Holy Ghost will bear record unto him of the Father and me; for the Father, and I, and the Holy Ghost are one" (3 Nephi 11:35-36). It is Jesus who defines the doctrines of His gospel not men, not councils, not opinions and decrees of men, not theological or philosophical pronouncements of men, but the Lord Himself who points the way for true converts to find eternal life in His church and kingdom. This is the message that our prospective members must come to know for themselves. They can, through the same process I did, the same process as outlined by Moroni.

Following my prayer that day in late October, I pondered these things carefully and then left my apartment and rushed back to the little seminary and institute building. I declared to John and Don'L Peterson, the institute director, that I wanted to be baptized. They were shocked. They said I would need the "lessons." I wondered why lessons were necessary as I recalled my sacred and powerful experience moments earlier. They persisted and said I would need the missionary lessons. I agreed that it was necessary to have the discussions. "Where are the missionaries that give these lessons?" I asked. They replied, "We don't know, but we will find out." The discussions were finally set for the next week with two missionaries, the first I had ever met. They taught me the formal missionary discussions and helped me set a baptismal date for November 17, 1962. Though only two weeks away, it seemed a long, long time for me.

BAPTIZE I bore my testimony in a small group at the Madsen home, during a gathering called a cottage meeting, the day before I was interviewed for baptism by an elder who was a district leader in the mission. I remember his wonderful demeanor as a servant of the Lord. My friend John Madsen baptized and confirmed me in Moscow, Idaho, some eight miles east of Pullman. My seminary classmates and Judith were in attendance. I had broken away from the traditions of the church fathers and my fathers. I had done as Jesus had done and as He asks all of us to do in His holy name.

I know God lives and has a divine plan for all of us. Can you see that the path to conversion is, in reality, not an event but a process of multiple changes that occur in our social and doctrinal awakening over a period of time? It goes on and on throughout our lives, even after baptism. We must understand this in order to understand our prospective members. This process of social and doctrinal change does not end with baptism. Baptism is often simply the beginning of the changes. As Nephi said, "Ye must press forward with a steadfastness in Christ, having a perfect brightness of hope, and a love of God and of all men. Wherefore, if ye shall press forward, feasting upon the word of Christ, and endure to the end, behold, thus saith the Father: Ye shall have eternal life" (2 Nephi 31:20). Surely it is a predicament of untold dimensions for the Lord to persuade a new convert to shed incorrect family traditions in order to bring eternal blessings to that same family for generations to come-not only that, but also to be able to bless past generations in that same family. All of this is truly a marvel to behold. The very family ties that become so strained as the convert approaches the new way of life are the same family ties that are carried to the temple over the years to be bound together by eternal ordinances. With my baptism, a modern-day pioneer had begun the long journey to the promised land of a sacred family search that would yet bless untold generations with the restored gospel. The despair that arose through the perceived breaking of family tied as a consequence of my baptism was overcome through faith in the Lord and trust in His teachings. I know "how great will be your joy" as I have partaken of the fulness of God's plan for His children!

I can think of few principles which I relish more than the principle of revelation. It is the tenet of my belief which fixes my hope on the Savior more than any other. I know He leads the Church. I am grateful beyond words for his latter-day prophets and apostles and other inspired leaders. What a pleasure it is to sit at their feet and partake of the fruits of contemporary revelation.

I have come into this Church because latter-day prophets have been called by God to do His work. I remember the year, the month, the day, and even the very moment when my heart encompassed the testimony that Joseph Smith was a prophet of God. He did the work of a prophet, and he was an instrument in the hands of God to make His will known on this earth again. There truly is a strait and narrow path which leads to eternal life by following the Savior and the living prophets. *We must accept them as the inspired trainers for our race of life.*

President C. (California Arcadia Mission, May 16, 1990):

"Fourteen missionaries arriving today. Whoops! Fifteen arrived. Sister D., a Spanish speaker, was not scheduled until next month, but we always have room for these wonderful missionaries.

She had arrived unexpectedly as a Spanish speaker and I had to place her with an English-speaking companion for one month.

I assigned her to a unit in the Hacienda Heights California Stake. *FIND* On the first day of tracting in their area with Sister L., she saw the home and family she had seen in a dream at the MTC! The family invited them into the back yard area where the sister had seen them in the spiritual prompting two weeks before at the MTC.

TEACH The family accepted the opportunity to be taught all the lessons, and a date for baptism. *BAPTIZE* The family was baptized 16 days later and Sister D. was transferred to another area the next week, to a Spanish-speaking Ward. The Lord did a wonderful job of putting that beautiful experience together!

7

The Joy Expands

It was the Monday after I was baptized a member of The Church of Jesus Christ of Latter-day Saints that I met my younger brother near the campus library. All of the family had fears of my joining the Church, and as I now approached Jerry, I sensed the first defense of my action. "Did you go through with it?" he asked. "Yes," I answered, "I was baptized Saturday night." We stood there looking at each other, searching for words that would be appropriate. "I feel good about what I have done," I said. Then he looked into my eyes and surprised me with his next remark: "You're my oldest brother. I know you wouldn't have done it if you didn't think it was right." A surge of relief flashed through me.

A few days later I was ordained a deacon in the Aaronic Priesthood, and I was serving in my first Church calling. My bishop was wonderful. He had sat down with me and discussed the need to extend to me a calling in the Church. I was stunned and surprised that this responsibility would come so soon. What a blessing it was to begin this nourishing process in the true church where everyone is needed to perform service to God and man. Imagine my trepidation as he stated the call to this twenty-one-year-old newly ordained deacon: "We feel inspired to invite you to serve as an Aaronic Priesthood quorum instructor." He assured me that another man would be with me as a member of the Young Men's presidency and that occasionally a member of the bishopric would sit in on our class to be of help. He gave me the manual of instruction and explained that lessons were prepared on different gospel topics and I would present one each week to the boys in the quorum.

As the school year began that fall, Jerry and I were both attending WSU. He was a sophomore and I was a senior. We both held campus jobs and were able to scrape together enough money each semester to enroll the following semester. Christmas vacation was approaching, and it was evident that there were not sufficient funds for either of us to continue in school unless some extra work was secured. We determined that we could work an extra week and thereby be able to stay in school. I invited Jerry to share my apartment with me since his dorm would be closed for vacation and my roommates would also be going home. *FIND* As we laid these plans, I kept thinking that perhaps the opportunity to share the gospel with him would become available. Then my plans hit a snag-he would work the night shift and I would work the day shift. We would be together only during breakfast and dinner hours.

How promising those hours became! Each day a new question was presented. Each day he would go visit the Catholic priest and ask him about the principles we had discussed. *TEACH* An interesting thing began to happen. At first the priest didn't take Jerry seriously, and he would come back to the apartment with his questions unanswered. Then the answers that were given could not satisfy Jerry's hunger for the truth. As each day passed, the pace quickened in the search for truth. He was eager to learn, and I was overjoyed at the opportunity to share my newfound love of the gospel with him. This Christmas vacation was turning out to be one of the most satisfying experiences of my life. It was an experience in giving and sharing that I shall never forget. After a week of these discussions and daily checking with his priest, Jerry declared, "I want to join your church. You have the answers to my questions."

Every waking hour was spent at the little table in the kitchen giving and receiving the simple witness that the gospel of Jesus Christ provides. Our meals were almost incidental compared to our feasting on the gospel message. We terminated our employment at the school near the end of December and boarded a bus for the half-day's ride home to be with our family. This trip was the shortest I have ever experienced, though I had traveled those miles many times. The things we shared made the time fly by so quickly. After we arrived at home, not much was said there about the fact that I had joined the Church. The mood of everyone was subdued, as if they were waiting to see what such an experience had done to me. I had a new appreciation for my family as I began to sense my responsibility to live my religion and share the gospel with them as I had been doing with Jerry. The beauties of the teachings of the Church and the profound doctrines of Christ are a foundation that is so helpful in our early days of conversion. I hearken often to the testimony of Helaman as he counseled his sons:

"Remember, remember that it is upon the rock of our Redeemer, who is Christ, the Son of God, that ye must build your foundation; that when the devil shall send forth his mighty winds, yea, his shafts in the whirlwind, yea, when all his hail and his mighty storm shall beat upon you, it shall have no power over you to drag you down to the gulf of misery and endless wo, because of the rock upon which ye are built, which is a sure foundation, a foundation whereon if men build they cannot fall" (Helaman 5:12).

Jerry and I returned to school early in January and continued to discover together the beauties of the restored gospel. *BAPTIZE* With his increased association with the restored gospel came the decision to join the Church, and he was baptized in March 1963 about 100 days after I had been baptized. What a day of joy it was for me! Now I was no longer alone in my separation from the family. We sat down after the baptism and rejoiced with each other about our hopes and concerns for our parents and brothers and sisters. Our bond as brothers in the gospel as well as brothers by mortal birth has been strengthened through each passing year. As a consequence of this great experience of gospel sharing that Christmas, I have never forgotten the impact of the responsibility to set the proper example to others in my family. Now we could grow together in the work of the Lord.

My learning did not stop with my baptism. It continued as I was given the responsibility of a calling to teach in an Aaronic

Priesthood quorum, the responsibilities of blessing the sacrament, and the member missionary responsibility to share the gospel message. This Church is not an idle man's church. We grow by being involved. That is the way of the Lord's gospel. I felt so grateful for all those who showed genuine interest in my participation and growth as a new member by offering me ways to be involved in the Church.

Elder C. (California Ventura Mission, October 2020):

"My companion and I were reopening an area called Santa Barbara. We had the same time in the mission and actually had been in the Mexico MTC together. When an area gets opened the missionaries usually don't have any information on the members or any potential investigators. This was right before quarantine and so we began to knock doors in an area that seemed like it had good potential. I specifically remember being nervous and a little stressed because neither of us had opened an area and we were both younger missionaries. I remember praying to be guided, comforted and relying on the Lord for help. *FIND* As we began to knock the 3rd door was a less active family who let us in and we began to teach the nonmember family member. After that lesson, a few doors later we knocked into a nonmember who was really good friends of a strong member in the branch. *TEACH* She had talked with missionaries before but she was finally ready to receive them again. We were guided to her and she progressed really well. Unfortunately COVID 19 started soon after. However, she continued to progress over videocalls and *BAPTIZE* was one of the first people in the mission to be baptized during quarantine. She is doing well and we stay in contact. It was such a sweet experience for me to realize the Lord was guiding me and I had no idea. The Lord guides us often in our lives and we often will never realize or recognize it. I will never forget this special experience I had on my mission."

8

Friends Know the Joy You Seek

What about our convert friends? Will we help them, love them, and nourish them—never giving up on them? Will we help sustain them through their trials, hardships, and difficulties as well as their joys? I regard my brother Gerald Scott Coleman, my first convert, as one of the most valiant of latter-day converts and a true friend to me. Since his conversion, we have been able to share a brotherhood of the highest respect and regard.

One year after his baptism, he was preparing to serve a mission. When the possibility of serving a mission was introduced to him, he did not think he could even consider the opportunity. His elders' quorum president told him that the quorum, his quorum, would provide the funds to allow him to serve a full-time mission for the Lord!

He accepted their most generous offer and soon he was called to serve in the France Belgium Mission, French speaking, and saturated with people who were members of the Catholic faith. FIND No problem for Elder Coleman. His door approach was most unique. Knock on the door. Wait for the person to open the door and declare they had no interest in the message from the Lord's servants. They would proceed to close the door. Elder Coleman would place his foot in the door opening. "I was a Catholic in my youth," he would declare. "We have a very special message for you from God and Jesus Christ."

Time and time again the French/Belgian people—individuals, couples, families, youth and acquaintances—would sense his sincerity and let him and his companion into their home. *TEACH* In his journal he has recorded teaching moments over and over again about the people he taught, baptized, confirmed, fellowshipped and ministered into the gospel of Jesus Christ. Couples from many walks of life were brought into the joy of the gospel. Mothers and children rejoiced in the missionary messages. Sometimes the families had been interested in the Church for years, and *BAPTIZE* Elder Coleman was able to help move them to joining the Church.

There were times when these faithful missionaries were asked by a priesthood leader to teach a part-member family that was not regularly participating in Church services. These missionaries brought one of the persons into the gospel, and the other person back to the gospel and the covenants made years before! Oh, what joy these converts exuded as they moved forward in the great joy of the restored gospel. Often the missionaries would be led by the Lord to people who had great love for Americans, who had helped liberate France during World War II. Is anything too hard for the Lord? Of course not! Elder Coleman sought to find those of God's children who had the blood of Israel in their veins and were open to the light and joy the elders shared with them.

Gerald and his wife, Susan, prepared their sons to serve as faithful missionaries. And now, another generation of their family members, their grandchildren, are going forth to serve the Lord and assist in the gathering of Israel to the restored gospel of Jesus Christ.

Just days after he returned from the mission field, Jerry was called to serve his country in the Vietnam War. He did so as a medic and as an ordained seventy. He taught the gospel in foxholes, bomb craters, and jungle camps and was regarded by his companions as a faithful and devout follower of the Lord. Miracles were part of this man's daily walk in the hazards of war.

Jerry and I have both served as bishops, in stake presidencies, and on high councils, and we have performed temple work for our deceased ancestors. I had the joy of ordaining him a patriarch in his stake! How I love faithful and obedient Gerald S. (Jerry) Coleman. To be with him, or hear his voice, or anticipate time together with him is one of my greatest joys in this life. I feel sweet nourishment from his faith and humble testimony and friendship. Jerry stood with me in my decision to join the Church. He still stands with me, and I with him. We are brothers in flesh and brothers in the gospel. Oh, what a difference dear friends and family make in a convert's ability to stay committed to the decision of baptism!

Helping converts build a solid foundation in the restored gospel will assist them in "never falling away." In this effort, we cannot underestimate the value of giving new converts the opportunity to serve in the Church.

Elder R. (California Carlsbad Mission, 2018-2019):

"In my first area it was kind of a rough area where we had very little communities of people. We were serving all we could just to talk to as many people as we could. I can't even count the things we tried.

"We got a phone call one morning while we were doing our studies. The lady on the phone was named Gail. Gail lived in Utah at the time but had been dating a man named Mike that just so happened to live in our area and wanted to know more about the Church. *FIND* He wanted to meet with us! It was a miracle we had been praying for. He asked if he could meet the next Saturday! We were so excited! That next Saturday we headed to his house and when we showed up he was outside and welcomed us; he was a total redneck! It was awesome! *TEACH* We went inside and sat down with him and he pulled out two Priesthood manuals, a Book of Mormon, a Bible, and a Preach My Gospel. He said these exact words, 'Just some of my reading material.' We were shocked. Mike was so prepared. Our prayers had been answered. We were able to get in multiple times a week and help them with stuff around their yard and spend time with them and teach Mike. Gail was a huge help in all of this. *BAPTIZE* We finally asked Mike if he would be baptized and he said yes! I had been praying and so had Gail that I would get one more transfer and the Lord blessed me with one more. My companion and I were on our way to the library to do our weekly planning on Friday the week before I was going to be transferred when we got a phone call from Mike that said we are gonna need some witnesses for the wedding we are having at my place tomorrow would you two be able to come? We were so excited! We were able to go the next day and be the witnesses for Mike and Gail's wedding at Mike's house. And the following Saturday I was able to baptize Mike and that next Monday I was transferred. It was truly a miracle. Hopefully one day they will be able to be sealed in the temple for eternity."

Elder Richard G. Scott has given excellent instruction on the joy of involvement and service:

"There are few things in life that bring as much joy as the joy that comes from assisting another to improve his or her life. That joy is increased when those efforts help someone understand the teachings of the Savior and that person decides to obey them, is converted and joins His church. There follows great happiness as that new convert is strengthened during the transition to a new life, is solidly grounded in truth and obtains all of the ordinances of the temple with the promise of all the blessings of eternal life" ("Why Every Member a Missionary?" *Ensign*, November 1997, 35).

We must nourish our converts by giving them real opportunities to serve in the Church. By doing so, we are offering them the chance to learn the gospel, deepen their testimonies, and find joy serving in the Lord's kingdom.

Sister C. (Brazil Porto Alegre Mission, 2012-2013):

"This week we went proselyting—one of my favorite things so far! My companion is from New Zealand but lived in Portugal for a year, and already knows quite a bit of the language so that is very helpful. We were on a very busy but small street in Sao Paulo. *FIND* In one hour, we placed three Livros de Mormon, a pamphlet and got two addresses of people who want to hear more/go to church.

It was the funnest experience. Brazilians loved it and were so receptive. I had a Book of Mormon in my hand and one man asked what it was and I gave it to him, and he lit up. They were very kind and patient with our language and very happy to receive a present from us. That was my line, 'presente para voce.' Or "a present for you today,' as I handed them a Book of Mormon. It was so neat to visit with these people—I love them so much and can't wait to speak more and teach. *TEACH* They wonder why we are so happy, haha.

"Honestly this is the happiest I've been in my life as I get to serve and have realized how blessed we are. Elder Uchtdorf said, 'To live with gratitude is to touch heaven.' Well, I am in heaven, here in Brazil. I thank and love you all tons."

Promptings from the Holy Ghost will also guide us to others who seek the true gospel. The Lord has said, 'I will be with you; and in whatsoever place ye shall proclaim my name an effectual door shall be opened unto you, that they may receive my word."

One morning, many years after my own baptism, I asked the Lord to help me find someone who could be introduced to the gospel. As I worked at the LDS Institute of Religion office all day, it was unusual for someone who was not a member of the Church to come and see me. Leaving the office, I thought about my earlier prayer and realized that I certainly had not been proactive in finding someone to visit with. While opening the car door, I noticed a young man standing by the fence some one hundred feet away. I hesitated and thought of my prayer again. The test of my faith was under way! Had the Lord raised up this person for me to meet, or was this just a coincidence? The moment came down to this: "Will you take a step of faith right now?" I have learned to pay attention to what some call "a divine rendezvous."

FIND Closing the door of the car, I walked up to the young man and introduced myself. He was friendly, easy to talk to, and a long way from home. He was a laborer on the remodeling project at the LDS Institute building where I worked. He was working there previous to entering Utah State University on an athletic scholarship. Was he a member of The Church of Jesus Christ of Latter-day

Saints? No. Did he know any members of the Church back in Arizona? Yes. Where were these friends now? They were on missions. Would he like to meet some of my college-age church friends who attended the Institute of Religion? Yes. Jason joined me for lunch at the Institute the following day and met many of my young church friends. He was beginning to find joy in the Lord.

In a few weeks Jason moved to Logan, Utah, to begin his university life. *TEACH* His institute director was alerted about this new student on campus. It was reported that Jason had been located and that he was living in one of the university dorms with returned missionaries as roommates. *BAPTIZE* It wasn't long before he called and invited me to his baptism. One year later he called again to invite me to his farewell preceding his mission. What a wonderful member! We have met his family and are so grateful for their progress in the Church. I know this is a work of helping our associates make important choices. Jason had made a choice. In fact, he had made a series of choices. He chose to listen to the message of the gospel. He awakened to principles of right and wrong and chose to seek the truth. He chose to commit himself to that same truth.

A few years ago I drove to Temple Square in Salt Lake City, Utah, to meet an acquaintance of the missionaries. Their guest did not keep the appointment. My response to the missionaries was, "The Lord will provide someone for us to teach." In less than two to three minutes, two adult men walked through the front door of the North Visitors' Center and directly up to us. They spoke Spanish, and we did not! *FIND* We assured them the best we could that someone would be able to help them. In moments, the only Spanish-speaking sister missionaries in the entire mission arrived at the visitors' center because they felt impressed to come there that morning!

TEACH Over a period of several weeks the missionary discussions were taught to those men, *BAPTIZE* and they asked to be baptized. The Lord was true to His word. "An effectual door" was opened in the very moment it was needed for this joyful experience.

After my baptism in November 1962, I was like a human sponge. I could not absorb enough of the truths of the restored gospel of Jesus Christ. The new doctrine, the clarity of the gospel, along with teachers and leaders who shared this influence with me were filling my cup to overflowing. I noticed that my new friends and leaders were often going to Lewiston or Moscow, Idaho for "leadership training." I wanted to go also, but I was not a leader. So, I asked if I could just ride along and learn from my peers by association. They took me with them to Lewiston. I would sit out in the car as the meetings began. On an occasion or two, someone would come outside and invite me to sit in the back of the chapel during the general training. Then they would dismiss to other more specific meetings. Again, someone would see me alone at the back of the chapel, in this unusual circumstance, and invite me to be part of one of the meetings going on in another room. It was glorious! I was learning and growing and finding my way into the Church. I was being nourished by the good word of God. It was like a constant spiritual rush to become acquainted with the scriptures, an expanding view of life, prophets, and eternity. So much clarity, purpose, and plainness flowed into me, things of power and light and truth that have changed my life for the good.

Elder R. (California Carlsbad Mission, 2018-2019):

FIND "In my third area there was a man named Ronnie. Ronnie's wife was a member of the Church but Ronnie was not. Ronnie is one of the best non-member members of the Church I have ever met. Ronnie was at church with his wife every single Sunday and was serving at the Church storehouse twice a week—he even served a service mission with his wife there for 2 years! And went on a 3-month Church history tour with his wife, just an incredible guy. Many many many missionaries have tried to get Ronnie to be baptized but were unsuccessful. Even I was. Ronnie had an issue with smoking. He did not want to get baptized then not be able to handle it and start smoking again and I have the utmost respect to him for that. We tried all we could to get him to stop and just do it. The stake president even went over to his house many many times to try and get him to be baptized but he said no. I knew that Ronnie would be baptized some day, he just wasn't ready yet *TEACH* so

I stopped trying to get him to be baptized and just was his friend and would talk to him whenever we saw him.

I left that area a few months later and finished my mission a few months after that in December of 2019. *BAPTIZE* About eight months ago, in August of 2020, I got a call from my companion at the time we were in that area with Ronnie and he told me that Ronnie had finally accepted to be baptized! I was able to zoom in and watch the baptism. It was truly a happy day for many many people in Ronnie's life and I am grateful to have been able to meet Ronnie and be one of the seeds that helped him get where he needs to be. It was an amazing experience."

9

Eternal Truths About the Family

S ome time ago my family and I were traveling across the state of Washington to visit relatives. At about the midpoint of our journey, I turned off the main highway and proceeded up a winding, narrow, dusty road to the old farm of my youth. The road was familiar, with its rocks and ruts and billows of dust that rolled up behind the car and spread out across the fields. The fields were familiar also, rolling for miles with endless patterns of green and brown woven together in a patchwork of beauty.

The children had never been to the old farm from that way before. It was fun for me to recall the memories and good times of climbing the great haystack rocks that protruded out of the field fifty to eighty feet high and still showed the boy-made monuments at their summit that we built years before. These huge rocks carried the white scars of lightning strikes and the aging of many years.

As I looked about, I recalled it was here where I had learned sacrifice and sharing with a large family. Here I had learned the principle of work. Here I had learned both to give and to receive of the labors of others. As a boy I had learned to pray with my family here. The old stove about which we gathered so many hundreds of times was gone also. It seemed that everything once so dear and beautiful was lost forever. Though the physical elements of our youth experiences were gone, we were building the foundation of our eternal family and the joy of being together forever in the next life.

Let me share another personal illustration on this matter of faith. When I was in a mission presidency in the Northwest, I had to travel to Seattle quite often to work with the president. On one occasion, as I drove there, I stopped in Issaquah, Washington where I called my "prospective member" sister from a phone booth. At that time I had been in the Church seven years.

"How's your family?" I asked. "They are doing great," she answered. "Do you love those kids?" I asked. "Yes," she replied. "Do you love your husband?" I inquired. "Yes," she responded. For seven years I had been searching for the key to her heart, because there is a key in every heart if we will strive to find it. Then my next question: "Are you going to be with him and your children forever?" A long pause. "Yes, I will," she said, "won't I?" And as she said "Won't I?" I knew the key to her heart! I knew what it was. I said, "I know the answer to that question, and Jerry and I will be happy to share it with you." I knew what would influence her to change. I knew that through her family we had found the key to her heart. Finally, after seven years, that was the key to sharing the gospel with her!

I was overjoyed at the prospect of bringing the gospel to her. I shared this zeal with my brother Jerry. We eagerly awaited the next development.

Several weeks later, I was attending a Zone Leader's Conference in Ellensburg, Washington. *FIND* The meeting was held on the second floor of the institute of religion. As I came to the head of the stairs and turned to go to the meeting room, I noticed an elder standing by the door. The spirit said, "That elder is going to baptize your sister."

I walked up to Elder M. I said, "Elder, you are going to baptize my sister." He said, Great! Where is she?" "She is in Graham, Washington." He said, "That's my area. That's where I work." I said, "Will you go see her?" "Yes," he said, "I'll be there tomorrow."

The next day Elder M. and his companion made a visit to my sister's home. Little Scotty, who was 4 years old at that time, answered the door. There was Elder M. and his companion. Elder M. and I look like brothers and I have a brother that looks like Elder M., too. So when 4 year old Scotty opened the door, he said, "Mama, Mama, Uncle Jerry is here!"

TEACH What a door approach! What more could an elder ask for? My sister came running to the door to see Uncle Jerry and it was the missionaries! BAPTIZE She and her husband were baptized a few weeks later. Jerry and I performed these ordinances.

Who touches the hearts? Who softens and changes the hearts? I know this is the Lord's work. I am grateful to be in it with you and I want to continue to do my share. The Lord will assist us in accomplishing success in this very important work.

You can bless families so much by sharing the gospel with them. The Lord has taught "for all men must repent and be baptized, and not only men, but women, and children who have arrived at the year of accountability" (D&C 18:42). The age of accountability has been defined by the Lord as eight years of age (D&C 68:27). The Lord further teaches the glorious doctrine with respect to children that "all children who die before they arrive at the year of accountability are saved in the Celestial Kingdom of heaven."

When we share the gospel with others, we begin to open the doors to eternity with our family. This is one of the most beautiful and hopeful doors we can open. Yet we also begin to help them close doors to traditions of the past. Because of the challenging nature of this task, we must be patient with the process of conversion. It is not an event. The way to help others is to show through our faith and their faith what God requires of them. "Lead me, guide me, walk beside me, help me find the way," says a cherished children's hymn. "Teach me all that I must do to live with him someday" is the plea for our little ones and converts who are asked to become as little children in finding their way back to God and the Lord Jesus Christ ("I Am a Child of God," *Hymns of The Church of Jesus Christ of Latter-day Saints* [Salt Lake City: The Church of Jesus Christ of Latter-day Saints, 1985], no. 301). One convert might come from one family, two from another, and even the whole family might be baptized in yet another instance. The sharing goes on, and each circumstance is different, private, even sacred.

In fast and testimony meeting Nancy shared this story, North Salt Lake Utah Stake, February 2021:

"Our son-in-law has a childhood best friend whose name is Jesse and his wife is Renae. They had a teenage son who suffered from cancer for a few years and passed away. This was so difficult and sad for Jesse and Renae. After a couple of years, they moved to a new area in California and decided they wanted to go to church. *FIND* On Facebook they asked if anyone had a church they could recommend. The missionaries very soon found their request and contacted them. *TEACH* They are now having the lessons and probably have attended church. They contacted our daughter and were very happy about them calling. *BAPTIZE* I was so happy to hear this story because this wonderful couple can now hear about the plan of salvation and know they can be with their son again and have a forever family."

Can you see why the Lord says there is joy in one who comes unto Christ and receives baptism in the true church? These things are true, and the Lord knows that we have the opportunity to be with our families and our loved ones forever, through all eternity. He knows what we must do to obtain this great blessing. We must come unto Him. We must commit ourselves to the gospel truth. We must be baptized and do all we can to bring this blessing into the lives of our friends and neighbors.

Elder B. (New York Syracuse Mission, January 2021):

"I testify that God never abandons us and He never will. Experiences in life are not meant to drag us down but to turn us to Christ who descended below them all so that He would know how to succor His people according to their infirmities. I know He lives and loves each of unconditionally!

FIND "This week was one for the books! *TEACH* We had a really cool couple of lessons with Larnell who is super solid *BAPTIZE* and so excited for his baptism on this Saturday! He has been reading the Book of Mormon every day the past week and he loves it. It's so cool to see how the Lord can change people into who He wants them to become! If you would have met Larnell one year ago, you would not recognize him as the same person! Because of Christ who is ready to receive you as you turn to Him, Larnell is a different person.

FIND "Theresa who was supposed to get baptized in December but didn't because life hit really hard and she had to deal with that for a while. *TEACH* We kept in touch with her through text but it was just hard for her so she wasn't responding. Then this past week when we called, she picked up! She said she had gotten all of our texts and they helped her get through her hard spot. She said she was feeling a lot better! She was able to go to church! We will be meeting with her again tomorrow to see how she's doing and how we can help! We are so excited for her! This experience taught me to keep trying and do what you can, you never know how your efforts are needed by others.

"We had good success with getting a hold of people who have been taught before by missionaries and we had some referrals work out too! The Lord moves His work forward in His way, His power, His timing. I know it's different for everyone and not every missionary is having these experiences but I thank my Heavenly Father every day for the blessings He has given me and for softening the hearts of the people here in Waukegan. His ways are perfect! As we align our will with His, our perspective changes and we will see His plan will always prevail! I know that to be true.

BAPTIZE "Last off, Roy got confirmed this week! Elder S. and I decided to give him one of our white shirts and some pants and a tie because the reason he didn't get confirmed last week was because he didn't have any clothes to wear and we didn't realize that. He loved our gift! It was so great to see him in slacks and a white shirt and tie at church. He and his family are doing good!

"I love you all! Thank you for the support and the Christmas letters! I wish I could call each of you and tell you how much I love and admire you! Keep moving forward! 2021 will be exactly what you make it to be, so let's make it a good one!"

Bringing converts unto Christ is a spiritual undertaking. It is also one of the trials of our faith. There are certain divine, eternal truths that God wants His children to hear. I believe that we all heard them before in the premortal gospel training we received. The truths we have known for eons of time may now be suppressed in mortality. They can be recognized, however, when the Holy Ghost stirs the depths of the soul and we hearken to the sweetness of the truths recorded on our eternal spirits. I feel this is what happens when we are brought to a circumstance of hearing the truths of the restored gospel. It is as though we have heard these things before and they are familiar to us. It is as though we have a longing to know the meaning and purpose of life. This longing can be satisfied only through learning the eternal truths encompassed in the gospel of Jesus Christ. President Joseph F. Smith taught, "All these salient truths which come home so forcibly to the head and heart seem but the awakening of the memories of the Spirit" (*Gospel Doctrine*, 5th ed. [Salt Lake City: Deseret Book, 1939], 13).

Anciently, Mormon wrote, "The Spirit of Christ is given to every man, that he may know good from evil; wherefore, I show unto you the way to judge; for every thing which inviteth to do good, and to persuade to believe in Christ, is sent forth by the power and gift of Christ; wherefore ye may know with a perfect knowledge it is of God" (Moroni 7:16).

The gospel of Jesus Christ is true. We enjoy the blessing of belonging to the only true church upon the face of the whole earth. Jesus Christ is our Savior, and it is His work that we share with others. Always the prophets have invited, even commanded us, to seek the Lord. "And now, I would commend you to seek this Jesus of whom the prophets and apostles have written, that the grace of God the Father, and also the Lord Jesus Christ, and the Holy Ghost, which beareth record of them, may be and abide in you forever" (Ether 12:41). We are led by living prophets who expound the restored gospel and teach us the way to eternal life through the Savior. I know the Book of Mormon is true, for I have received the witness promised in the writings of Moroni. Joseph Smith was indeed a prophet of God.

May we sincerely pray that the Lord will help us share these truths with family and friends. May we bear testimony to those whom we fellowship that we have a precious gift that will change their lives and bring them great joy. May we take courage to bring converts to Christ. Now is the time to share the gospel message and spread the good news of the Restoration. Now is the time to help our friends and neighbors grow in the gospel both before and after baptism, so that they too can experience the eternal joys that the truth can bring.

In his very first message as a newly-ordained Apostle, Elder Russell M. Nelson at the April 1984 General Conference of the Church spoke of the gathering of Israel in these latter days. He said,

"I testify that we are of the house of Israel, specifically of the lineage of Joseph, bearing the birthright and charged with the irrevocable responsibility to prepare the world for the second coming of the Savior. Then, numberless multitudes among every nation, kindred, tongue, and people will eventually join in proclaiming that Jesus is the Christ, the Son of the living God" (*Ensign*, May, 1984).

The process of being "gathered into the House of Israel" had begun for me, as a college student in Pullman, Washington. Inasmuch as I partook of the great blessing of being baptized into The Church of Jesus Christ of Latter-day Saints on 17 November 1962, I therefore was among those "gathered to Israel" in the last days. Eighty-nine days later I received my Patriarchal Blessing wherein the Patriarch declared that "you are of the blood of Joseph through his son Ephraim. This brings you the promises of the blessings of Abraham, Isaac and Jacob. It was through the blood of Israel that you were gathered out of the world and brought to a knowledge of the truth."

No one should be surprised at the teachings of this Prophet of our day as he spoke to the youth of the Church in June 2018. He exhorted the young people "to enlist in the youth battalion of the

Lord" and take part in "the *greatest* challenge, the *greatest* cause, the *greatest* work on earth." That challenge is the gathering of Israel.

"There is *nothing* of greater consequence ... this *is* the mission for which you were sent to earth." He further invited the youth to participate in this great latter-day work with the following words: "Would you like to help gather Israel during these precious latter days?" (Russell M. Nelson and Wendy W. Nelson, "Hope of Israel," Worldwide Youth Devotional, June 3, 2018.)

Elder R. (Illinois Chicago Mission, 2020-2022):

FIND "A few miracles this week. First off the Lord directs His work. We make plans every day but the Lord is really the one in charge. So on Friday we made plans and literally everything we planned to do didn't happen. But it was the best day of the week because He provided so many miracles! We got a hold of Theresa who we've been trying to get a hold of all week and were able to help her with a problem she was having which was cool! Then a member lesson got pushed back half an hour and right when we were supposed to have that lesson with them we got a call from Latasha who we've tried to get a hold of all week too! She was having a rough time with her family and was stressed and panicking a little but she went to a place she could be alone and talk to us and we were able to calm her down and show God's love for her and how she truly is never alone. The Spirit was so strong and it went to show me the Lord cares a lot about His children!

"We met with Larnell (recent convert) and his friend Roger (non member) which was cool! *TEACH* We introduced the Book of Mormon to him and he loved it. We are going back over this week!

"Tony has been looking into the Church for a while and we had a cool lesson with him about Joseph Smith and the first vision and how the Book of Mormon plays a role into all of that and the Spirit was super strong. He said he just doesn't want to commit to anything but we are working with him! Lots of cool things are happening!"

Please study carefully the enclosed "The Family: A Proclamation to the World" document which is a latter-day witness of the sacredness of the eternal family unit (Appendix III).

10

Invite Them to Come In or Come Back

We invite people of all walks of life to join this Church. Why? Because the Lord directs this work and he desires that the great message of the restoration of his gospel be taken to every person. He has said:

"I command all men everywhere to repent ...

"Remember the worth of souls is great in the sight of God;

"For, behold, the Lord your Redeemer suffered death in the flesh; wherefore he suffered the pain of all men, that all men might repent and come unto him.

"And he hath risen again from the dead, that he might bring all men unto him, on conditions of repentance.

"And how great is his joy in the soul that repenteth.

"Wherefore, you are called to cry repentance unto this people" (Doctrine and Covenants 18:9-14).

The worth of souls is great! All people everywhere are the children of God. This Church has been commissioned and authorized to bring the message of salvation to all people. We do not do it by virtue of popularity and convenience. We are commanded to do so. God is no respecter of persons. He loves Catholics, Protestants, Jews and non-believers equally. He commands us to take the restored gospel of Jesus Christ to everyone. He is concerned that all men, no matter what tradition of religion they espouse, should hear the correct message of salvation.

As our missionary forces spread out across the earth, these men and women seek to teach the gospel to all those who are honest in heart and who seek the truth. In particular, our efforts are directed towards bringing families into the Church. Since families are greatly strengthened by the gospel, we are especially anxious to to encourage fathers and heads of families to join the Church and lead their families upon the gospel path.

Elder B. (Uganda Kampala Mission, October 2019):

"...Anyways onto the spiritual part, day 2 was by far the hardest day I have had in a very long time. We had awful jetlag so we were all so exhausted. On top of that everyone in my district seemed so far ahead of me in everything. I didn't have a laundry bin or all these little things and I was just so tired and angry with myself, thought of 'why am I even here' and 'I am just going to hold these people back and get in the way I have no place here' so I prayed for some kind of confirmation that I individually was meant to be where I am and I got it. That night in our big MTC devotional they called the district leaders and all was well I was sitting there very discouraged, when I heard my name read and I was told to stand, I hadn't been listening and was very confused because all the district leaders had already been called, then I heard the words 'Zone Leader.' Tears instantly began to come to my eyes because I knew that I had received the calling from my Heavenly Father to help me specifically with that. It is crazy because I am the Zone Leader of the whole MTC and it's been such an amazing experience for me. Ever since then every day has flown by and things are always looking up."

The Book of Mormon is used as the principal tool in our search for investigators. We love the Bible and use it daily, but the Book of Mormon is the keystone of our religion. When a person reads it, ponders it, and prays about it, the Lord prepares his mind for bursts of inspiration and testimony that testify it is true. It is true, and Joseph Smith brought it forth by the inspiration of God. A man recently asked me why he saw our missionaries carrying the Book of Mormon with them so frequently. "Don't you believe in the Bible?" he asked. I replied that we do believe in and use the Bible, but the Book of Mormon is the key to conversion. It points the way to latter-day revelation, prophets, and the restoration.

Elder B. (Uganda Kampala Mission, 2018-2020):

"It seems strange that one year ago exactly I was serving in Ntinda Uganda which is a district within the Uganda capital city of Kampala in which we decided to go Christmas caroling in the poorest district of the city called Kisugu (pronounced Juh-soo-goo). It was in Kisugu I saw some of the greatest poverty the world has to offer, there was no snow or hot chocolate, there was no shopping sprees for gifts, there was no Christmas trees or red and green lights, but despite all of these things it was the greatest Christmas of my life. Why? Because what they did have was a heart and mind focused on the Savior. I remember seeing these impoverished people many of which had no shoes nor shirts, weep at the less than perfect songs of us few missionaries, they were weeping for joy because of their faith and love of Jesus Christ and God, they wept because they knew that it was because of Him that they can return to their Father in Heaven, they wept because they trusted God to the point that they KNEW that all would be made right because of Him. At this time it is so important to remember the birth of our Savior and all the blessings that would follow this birth and I hope this Christmas is a good one for everyone who reads this because it's an unusual year and this Christmas will be unforgettable so may as well make it a good unforgettable one right? I just wanted to finish in saying I know God lives and loves us individually. God sent Jesus Christ for all mankind yes that is true but sometimes we forget that God sent Him for you specifically, He came so that you could return and I know this is true and I bear that witness in the name of Him, Jesus Christ, amen."

The testimony recorded within the pages of this humbly written effort is penned by the power of conviction. The thoughts and principles are rooted deep in my soul. The truths are from an eternal source, unyielding and ever reliable. The ability to portray them accurately and properly is a struggle of great magnitude, not because the gospel is not plain and simple but because no words are forceful enough, not sufficiently convincing in and of themselves, to move men or women to prepare to meet their Maker.

Please rejoice with me and these converts I have known during my years in the Church as a member missionary.

I taught an Old Testament Adult Religion class. Jim and Janie enrolled. I soon learned that Janie was a Latter-day Saint but that Jim was not. He appeared to be a little reluctant to become involved in a religion class but he attended quite faithfully as each succeeding month went by. Several weeks into the course, I met Jim and Janie at the door of the classroom. After greeting them and shaking hands, I began an experiment. "Jim," I said, "I sure hope you will invite me to your baptism!" He responded, "I'm not going to be baptized! I'm not interested in joining the Mormon Church!" I gently said, "I know, but just in case you ever want to join, please invite me to your baptism." Jim just laughed and proceeded into the classroom.

FIND Our class met for thirteen weeks. Nearly every week I would quietly ask Jim to be sure to invite me to his baptism. There were occasions when we visited in my office while he asked questions he had about the gospel. Near the end of the course I called upon him one evening to give the opening prayer. He did a fine job. Having heard other members of the class pray each week, he had learned the pattern of prayer from them. Again, after the class, I quietly thanked him for giving such a good prayer and asked him if he would invite me to his baptism someday. Finally the last class was held and we were all to part and go our separate ways for the summer. As I shook hands with each of the class members, and as I tidied up the classroom, I noticed that one person remained behind. He nervously paced the hall outside the classroom waiting for me. As I stepped Into the hall, he asked if he could see me in my office for a few minutes. I asked, "How can I help you, Jim?" TEACH His long-awaited response was, "Brother Coleman, do you think you could arrange for me to be taught the gospel and be baptized? I feel I am ready!" It was with joy that I picked up the phone and called the ward mission leader in his ward boundaries. In moments the arrangements were made for him to have his first appointment with missionaries. *BAPTIZE* A few days later I received a phone call "Brother Coleman," Jim said, "I have chosen a date for my baptism. I would like you to be there if you can arrange It."

Is anything too hard for the Lord? Obviously not! But He does much of His work through His Church and its members.

Very often member missionary work we participate in is right before us among family members and friends with whom we are now acquainted. We find that there are many occasions where a prospective member has never been committed to baptism because we have feared that somehow our actions will bring about a great crisis in this person's life.

Such was the case with Mary, a wonderful Catholic woman married to Bill, an active Church member. *FIND* Mary had been taught the missionary discussions many times but she had avoided the final step of baptism. As I visited with her one afternoon she did not seem to be against joining the Church, but rather she was not yet convinced that she should go ahead with this important decision. *TEACH* It appeared she was ready, though not sufficiently committed to set a date to follow through with baptism.

I asked Bill if he thought his wife was ready for baptism. He agreed that he was very much in favor of her taking this step but that the decision must be hers. I called their bishop and arranged for the time and date for Mary's baptism, only four days hence! Those four days passed quickly for this lovely couple and their children. *BAPTIZE* After twenty years of involvement in The Church of Jesus Christ of Latter-day Saints, they were finally at the edge of the baptismal waters. Bill would perform this sacred ordinance for Mary. They radiated the peace and happiness of this special time. Friends and family members felt blessed to witness this significant step of faith by Mary and her husband.

There are many persons in this Church today who have left home, family, and friends for the gospel. The change in their lives has been profound and marvelous.

FIND I recall ministering to a family where the wife was said to have been a member and the father a prospective member. After my companion and I had visited with the father a number of times, he said that he really didn't understand why we continued to visit their family. "After all," he said, "my wife isn't a member, and if she is, I will leave her right here and now!" Oh what grief swept through our hearts as we witnessed her sorrow and tears at that moment. What was to be done? How could we give comfort and aid in such a difficult circumstance?

It was true. His wife was not a member of the Church. Through a set of unusual events several years before, she had "almost" been baptized and subsequently her name had appeared on the rolls of the Church. As we later evaluated the situation, the Bishop felt we should continue to visit the home subject to the father's approval. *TEACH* It seemed he would never soften his heart and let us teach him about the gospel. But gradually we found things to interest him and we began to see a change of heart.

Late one night as I lay asleep, I received a phone call from this prospective member. *BAPTIZE* "Brother Coleman," he asked, "are you busy Friday evening?" Still groggy with sleep, I asked what I could do for him. "Would you baptize my wife and me on Friday? It's my birthday and I want it to be a special occasion!"

Who cannot change? Who cannot be rescued? It would have been easy to label this man as a hopeless missionary effort. What change can God wrought in the hearts of men!

Through the scriptures we find ourselves, and we discover our true nature. We discover that our total dependence is upon the Lord for becoming what we may become. We find in the scriptures the formula for becoming new creatures, for overcoming the world, for exercising the power of faith.

As we search the scriptures and desire to live by the principles therein, we are re-committed to the power of righteousness and obedience as opposed to the destructive forces of unrighteousness and disobedience.

Mark had been a Catholic Monk. He was raised for six years in a Catholic orphanage run by a group of Franciscan Nuns and spent four years at Boys' Town in Omaha, Nebraska. After spending several years in the Navy, Mark began to study to be a Catholic priest. He labored in this vocation for several years but felt something was missing in his quest to serve Jesus Christ. He became a monk thinking that further sacrifice and service were needed to bring the feelings of peace and contentment he desired. Again, he felt something was missing. He had a series of dreams that caused him to wonder and search for happiness.

As Mark sought purpose to his life, he resolved that this could only be accomplished by isolating himself from all elements of society and material possessions and becoming a hermit. He thought surely this would bring him closer to God. He made preparations for a life that would take him into the hills and away from human contact once and for all.

FIND But then came the day when someone knocked at his door. Mark opened it. There stood two Church missionaries. He turned them away but he watched them from his window as they went from one door to another, being rejected by each person they called upon. He thought to himself, "Here I am going up into the mountains to find the love of God, and here are these two young men walking around the streets with it!" As the missionaries came back down the street, Mark went out into his yard and asked them for a pamphlet. They gave him one called *Christ in America*. They also asked if they could call on him again, to which he replied that they could if they wanted to.

TEACH Mark read the tract. He had never heard such a message. He hoped the missionaries would come back. They did and that began a search for truth that Mark could not leave alone. He soon discovered that the Prophet Joseph Smith had been the central character in the many dreams he had been experiencing for the past 15 years. *BAPTIZE* After much study and prayer, Mark joined the Church.

Who can change? A simple tract, the humble act of giving to another, opened the heart of a man who was searching for peace and purpose in his life.

Another popular member missionary approach has been through the use of the Book of Mormon as a tool in introducing a prospective member to the Church. Many suggestions have been offered on how to stimulate interest in this book and on how to prepare people for further missionary contact. Over the years Church leaders have learned that the Book of Mormon had accounted for less than one per cent of the initial contact regarding the Church. It is obvious that use of the Book of Mormon must therefore accompany a personal relationship with the prospective member involved in order to maximize the success.

Elder C. (Washington DC South Mission, 2018-2019):

FIND "While serving in Northern Virginia, my companion and I had the blessing of meeting a Latino family. A couple of elders that did not speak Spanish had knocked their door, spoken with them briefly, and sent their information over to us. We strongly felt like we needed to go see them right away. Noemi and her son Jefferson greeted us at the door and Noemi explained she had been begging God to send people that would help teach her son about the gospel.

"We sat down with their family and introduced to them the Book of Mormon and how it related to what they already understood about the Bible. Jefferson enjoyed reading from the Book of Mormon and Noemi could see that it was helping Jefferson come closer to God, but she struggled to read from it herself. TEACH We realized that reading and understanding the scriptures was a challenge for her and it was making it difficult to help them attend church with us as a family. Noemi would read, but not understand anything from the stories, and couldn't remember anything we read together.

"For several days my companion and I had prayed that Noemi would be blessed with the ability to read and understand the scriptures. Following days of heartfelt prayer and several emotional visits with the family, we visited again and found that overnight Noemi had been blessed with the ability to read the scriptures and see how it connected personally to her life. She quickly developed a testimony of the Book of Mormon which motivated her to attend church where she felt comfortable and loved. She motivated Jefferson to read daily, and actively participate with the other youth at church. *BAPTIZE* Shortly after, Noemi and Jefferson were baptized.

"I still cry every time I think about the miracle that the Lord performed in the home of this beautiful family. I know and testify that the Lord can bestow knowledge and spiritual gifts. I'm grateful to have seen such a tender and powerful miracle in the lives of my friends I love so dearly."

FIND I remember sharing a Book of Mormon with a young man in a college dormitory. I called upon him in his dorm when I was teaching at the Institute of Religion at an adjacent college. He was quite cynical about my visit and my attempt to become his friend.

TEACH Eleven years after we met, I was in the Moses Lake, Washington Stake center in the Northwest when he came up to me and said, "Do you remember me?" Fortunately I did and I was thrilled to see him. He introduced me to his wife and said he would like to share something with me. He said that he had thought about our visit in his dorm for several years and based on that brief contact and his reading and study of the Book of Mormon, *BAPTIZE* he and his wife had joined the Church! Imagine that kind of success from a mere gesture of caring and sharing with this man years before.

FIND A young lady who has been attending the Mutual activities in our ward came to me recently and asked, with tears streaming down her face, if she could be baptized. *TEACH* She had already secured her parents' permission to be taught the gospel in her home. *BAPTIZE* The youth and leaders of the ward had drawn her into the love of the gospel by being her friend.

We should be able to open a missionary door under almost any circumstance if we are willing to do so.

We may never know of the success that can come from seeds we plant in fertile soil; yet plant the seeds we must, year after year. Planting seeds one time is not sufficient. We must try again and again. We must continue to involve ourselves in missionary efforts so that, one day, we may realize the harvest.

Several years after a young couple had been married, the mother of the wife called to ask if I would visit the couple and encourage the husband to join the Church. There have been times when such requests have made me feel uneasy at best. I often wonder why others think I have more courage to tackle such a situation than they have.

I called the young mother and searched for a comfortable way to make the acquaintance of her husband. Already fears were preying on my mind. "Why should I do this? I don't even know this man. What am I doing trying to set up a missionary appointment? What if he isn't interested at all and I'm just going to make a fool of myself?" Fears and doubts came flooding in. Barriers were starting to come up. Nothing had even happened but I sure was anticipating problems.

I pushed fears and doubts and barriers aside and the first appointment was scheduled. I asked a young man who was preparing for his mission to accompany me to the home. We knocked and waited. We knocked again. No one was home. What did that mean? New doubts rushed into my mind. "See, he didn't really want to meet with us. He probably thinks we are imposing our religion on him and he wants nothing to do with us."

FIND I phoned the couple the next day. The wife was very apologetic about not being home when we visited. "My husband had to work," she said. "Can we set another appointment?"

The same doubts and fears started to build again, but faith prevailed and for a second time my companion and I climbed the stairs to the little apartment. We knocked and waited. The door opened and there stood the "prospective member." *TEACH* He was polite, kind, attentive and—most of all—teachable. Doubts and fears quickly melted away as I realized that he truly was receptive to the gospel message; that he wanted to know more about his young wife's faith.

Thereafter, we enjoyed several successful discussions. *BAPTIZE* Full-time missionaries completed the discussions and baptized him.

Elder C. (American Samoa, 1991-92):

"As I have reflected on my time as a missionary in Samoa, my mind has continually returned to the role that sporting and manual labor played in my missionary efforts. For many months of my mission I worked in areas considered very remote, even lacking running water. In some of those areas I was the only white-skinned visitor in two decades, at least so much as staying long enough to get to know anyone, let alone preach the Restored Gospel.

"Most Samoans and their villages were highly Christianized. But most villages had a favored religion. If the chief was powerful, there would often be less choice among the faiths, as villagers were often expected to maintain harmony by assuming the religion held by the chief. Thus, mine was a minority religion that the village chief and witch doctor usually frowned upon. Formal teaching was often prohibited.

"Here is where sporting such as boxing and rugby, and working in the plantations to plant and harvest taro, ta'amu, and other starchy plants played a pivotal role in introducing these sweet people to the Restored Gospel. I loved throwing a rugby ball with village youth. And for a time I was a trainer of a local boxing club that had Olympic aspirations. I would wake up at 4:30 am to run with the young men on the single paved road that ran only a few yards from the black rocky beach.

"After we worked a day in the plantations, in the evenings many in the village would gather to listen to me tell what they called "the beautiful stories," about astronaut trips to the moon, the principles of levers and inclined planes, and the restoration of the gospel taught to a young prophet of Jesus Christ.

"My heart still wells with love and a feeling of heavenly mercy for this singular opportunity I had to connect with people that live on a little island at the very edge of each day's last light. When morning hits mere moments later, it lands where my eldest sister and her husband now serve east of Asia in the Philippines."

As our son K. concluded his mission in the Pacific Islands, he shared with us the great difficulties he experienced there. Years later he had the great joy of assisting his son to come into the Church. *FIND* His seventeen-year-old son had been searching online for information about churches and in particular The Church of Jesus Christ of Latter-day Saints! He told his father that he wanted to join the Church. *TEACH* Our son was overjoyed with this news. He pledged to his son that he would prepare himself to perform the ordinances of baptism and confirmation in the true Church.

BAPTIZE On February 14, 2015 our family drove and flew to the city where the ordinances would take place and we all witnessed the great joy for a father, son, siblings, cousins, nephews, and parents! Father and son grew together in the gospel once again. Our son prepared to be remarried and he and his wife were sealed in the Portland Oregon Temple, and I was the sealer for this sacred ordinance. Soon his son was preparing to serve a full-time mission. He was a valiant missionary, deeply committed to service among the Spanish-speaking population of the Washington DC South Mission.

Is this not pure and beautiful joy in those whom we invite to come in and those we invite to come back to the glorious gospel of Jesus Christ! Our family rejoices always to have this eternal family, all of our children born in the sealing covenant of temple marriage, and all our children and grandchildren having entered into these sacred covenants also. Now let us rejoice in the blessings from the Lord.

My wife shared the following experience with me regarding her friends and associates. *FIND* A few years ago she went to her high school library and reviewed the names of those who had *TEACH* checked out a copy of the Book of Mormon that had been on the shelves. And she learned that very significant things had happened to two of those whose names were on the book checkout card. Either the person who had checked out the Book of Mormon *BAPTIZE* had eventually joined the Church, or a member of the family of the person who checked out the book had joined the Church! The person or persons who placed that Book of Mormon in the school library probably do not even know of the good they did with this small act of sharing and service. Imagine the stories of conversion and happiness that came out of this step of faith.

If I make one hundred referrals per year and one, two, four or ten result in baptisms, have I failed because I didn't have success with one hundred? Of course not! I had success with one, I had more success with two. It is very difficult to fail if my possibilities for success are greater.

Hundreds and hundreds of ideas are offered in Church magazines, pamphlets, brochures, talks, and personal experiences to illustrate approaches to missionary work. Any of these may work for you. Or you may have an approach that no one else has heard of or tried.

Member missionary work is very personal. If you have the gospel, if you have a desire to share the gospel, you have the tools to be a member missionary. You don't have to be like Brother So and So, or Elder Successful, or Sister Personality, you just have to do what you do best. You may not even have a "gimmick," or an "approach," or even be able to quote scripture. Remember the Lord asked us to love our neighbors. Becoming acquainted with them is the key in sharing the gospel with them!

Sister C. (Utah Provo Mission, November 4, 2013):

"We got a call from a man named Westley who introduced himself and said, 'I've been baptized but I haven't been to church in about 10 years. My wife isn't a member, and we were wondering if we could have the missionary discussions?' We couldn't believe it. We set up an appointment with them and we were so excited to meet this family!

FIND "A few days later we met with them and learned that Wes was raised in the Church but left when he was 18, and Lacy was raised Baptist. They had two little girls and they wanted to know more about the Church and whether or not it's true. Even though we'd prepared for the lesson, we were having a difficult time teaching and it wasn't going smoothly. There were many interruptions and I kept having thoughts come to my mind like, 'this family won't want to meet again,' and 'the Spirit isn't here.' My companion later shared that she was experiencing the same thoughts. It was discouraging, but thankfully they did set another appointment. Our next lesson went well, and as we prepared for a third lesson we prayed about how we could invite Lacy to be baptized. *TEACH* We felt inspired to teach the Plan of Salvation. As we testified of eternal families the Spirit filled the room, and Lacy tearfully shared with us that her mom (who was Baptist) had passed away. She'd never been taught that she could be with her family after this life, and she was grateful to hear that everyone (including her mom) will have the opportunity to accept the gospel, whether in this life or the next. Lacy agreed to pray about being baptized. We prayed and fasted for this family and they started coming to church.

BAPTIZE "On November 18th, Lacy told us that she wanted to be baptized and less than two weeks later she became a member of The Church of Jesus Christ of Latter-day Saints. One year later they were sealed as a family in the temple, and they've grown to be a family of six. Their oldest daughter Emma was baptized earlier this month (February 2021)."

Elder Dale G. Renlund has taught with respect to joy in the gospel, "Our Savior wants to forgive because this is one of His divine attributes.

"And, like the Good Shepherd He is, He is joyful when we choose to repent…

"Repentance is not only possible but also joyful because of our Savior…

"I invite you to feel more joy in your life: joy in the knowledge that the Atonement of Jesus Christ is real; joy in the Savior's ability, willingness, and desire to forgive; and joy in choosing to repent" (General Conference, October 2016).

As you share these beautiful principles of joy in the gospel of Jesus Christ with your friends who love their family, you will open the doors of eternity and eternal families to them. They will be grateful to you forever.

11

Keep Sharing Your Joy in the Gospel

P resident Dallin H. Oaks of the First Presidency of the Church recently spoke to a New Mission President's Seminar and said, "Convert baptisms have plateaued. We must find new ways to do missionary work that will bring the increases in missionary baptisms of which we are capable" (Mission President Seminar, June 2017, Provo, Utah).

Have you ever wondered why we struggle to begin missionary work even after we feel really motivated to do something, such as after an especially inspirational conference or Sacrament meeting?

Let's analyze a typical member missionary situation.

We live the gospel and demonstrate our faithfulness by regular attendance at our meetings. We carry out our assignments, hold a temple recommend, and pay our financial obligations in the kingdom. We sit in an inspirational meeting where our heart has definitely been touched regarding missionary work. We think of a neighbor, a friend, even a relative with whom we would really like to share the gospel. We resolve in our heart that we will make an honest and courageous effort to meet with our "prospective member" acquaintance as soon as possible. The closing hymn is sung, the benediction is offered. We leave the meeting and head home. We think about the person we are going to visit with about the gospel. And we wonder what approach would be best.

A thought enters into our mind and it goes something like this: "Maybe this isn't the time to talk to so and so about the gospel," or "I wonder if so and so would think I'm being too over-bearing if I impose my religious views on him," or "They will probably laugh at me when I bring up religion," or "I wonder If I could answer their questions," ... excuses unending.

By the time we get to the car or walk a block or two toward home, thoughts of doubt are flooding into our mind. Perhaps these doubts take the following pattern: "Good grief, so and so has just had that problem come up. He wouldn't want to hear about the gospel now. I'd better hold off awhile," or "I hate to bother so and so about religion, she would think I'm crazy or something," or "I wish I knew the scriptures better, then I could defend my beliefs better," or "I don't know what approach would be least offensive to them and I'd better back off until I'm sure of what to do."

By the time we get home our thoughts are: "Well, that was a great meeting. Brother so and so really has had great experiences and he shared wonderful ideas: Someday I'd sure like to do my duty and bring a family into the Church, but right now I'm just not prepared."

What has happened here? Why were we ready to get involved twenty minutes ago and now we are right back were we were before the meeting? Did someone physically stop us from doing what we wanted to do? Did someone confront us on the street or in the car and threaten us if we carried out our missionary effort? Of course not. But something changed our mind. What was it?

Sister L.(Brazil Florianopolis Mission, 2009-2011):

10/2009 Itajai, Brazil: "In my first area of Itajai, Brazil I found myself with my trainer in a scarier part of town. The homes were cramped, makeshift huts, with dirt roads and not much electricity in the area. It was dark, there weren't many streetlights and it was getting close to curfew. I was definitely scared and I let Sister P. know and she replied, 'Sister L., we are doing the Lord's work and He will take care of us.' That really hit me and I believed it. I wasn't scared again for the rest of my mission. Looking back there are places we worked that I wouldn't go back to as an everyday person, but as a messenger of the Lord with a tag on I knew that I was taken care of.

2010 Balneario Camboriu, Brazil: "This area was so interesting in the fact that we never had success street contacting or knocking on doors. But, almost EVERY SUNDAY someone would show up at the church inquiring about the Church and wanting to learn more It was crazy. We had Valdervino, who worked on Sundays and lived near the chapel. *FIND* He told the Lord that when he didn't work on Sundays anymore that *TEACH* he would go to 'that church' to find out what it was all about. His work scheduled changed so he didn't work on Sundays and he came to learn and was *BAPTIZE* baptized. One of my most favorite families is Joao, Vanesa and their 13-year-old daughter, Sabrina. *FIND* Vanesa had been searching for a church for a long time and Joao was just supporting her. They came to the church as a recommendation from a family member who knew a member. *TEACH* On our second lesson we felt impressed to invite them to be baptized and crazy enough Joao accepted before Vanesa felt she was ready! Joao had read the Gospel Principles booklet and said it all made sense and that he believed it. *BAPTIZE* Joao was baptized first, received the priesthood and then baptized Vanesa and Sabrina. It was pretty fantastic. I accredited our efforts throughout the week, though they seemed fruitless, it resulted in Sabbath Day blessings. Blessings don't generally come immediately and for me, they always come in a way I never expect."

Sometimes we allow our desires to do missionary work to be overcome by Satan's intimidation of our thoughts! All that needs to happen to stop us in our tracks is for us to anticipate failure, ridicule, or hurt feelings. The greatest motivation in the world will never get us anywhere until we quit listening to our negative self. We "put down" our own efforts and we never really get the Lord involved in the process of breaking through the approach avoidance barrier in our mind. If we listen to our negative self, we feel we can't do the work the Lord wants us to do.

Yet the Prophet teaches us we can. Our negative self teaches us we can't walk through an open missionary door and the Lord teaches us we can, by faith. Through our negative thoughts, we teach ourselves that our self-image will somehow be attacked or bruised if we do member missionary work. The Lord teaches us not to fear man but to trust in the Lord. So who is controlling our efforts when we don't try to have missionary success? We allow (and we have to take responsibility for this) ourselves to experience fear and doubt and this condition is not inspired by the Lord!

Sister C. (Alabama Birmingham Mission, 2012-2013):

"Good good week! So Ingrid is going to be getting baptized this Saturday!!! She has family coming up from Miami, and she is so excited. *FIND* We saw her almost every night this week and even had a Temple Square sister from Honduras come and meet their family. That was fun. *TEACH* She is learning so much and accepting everything. She loves the conference talks, and was able to share her testimony of living prophets to her in-laws. *BAPTIZE* Sister B. and I were talking about how we haven't done anything, it is all the Lord, we show up and He teaches her. We love going though because her 2-year-old and 1-year-old scream 'MUCHACHAS!!' whenever we come. Makes us feel loved. Haha

"Paco is doing really well. He received the priesthood yesterday and he is just so happy. He wants us to come over all the time too. Haha. We are preparing him to go to the temple the 28th of June. He is excited.

"We played soccer Friday and we had some investigators from both of the branches show up, somehow they convinced both Sister B. and I to play. That was a treat.

"A family got baptized in the branch this week! A mom and her two kids, she has two others as well. It was so exciting, she has friends and family come, and we were able to meet some great people and talk to a less-active who she is friends with and hadn't been to church in 15 years! It was a beautiful day!

FIND "The Lord has a lot of ready people here, so we are busy with the other missionaries trying to see them, set up appointments and follow-up. There is a lot to do. I was on exchanges this past Saturday and we found some new investigators for their teaching pool. We explained the apostasy like a puzzle, losing some of the pieces and they said it totally made sense. *TEACH* One of them actually has family members who are members of the Church. We almost didn't stop to talk to them because we were running late. So glad we did! That is one thing our mission president is pushing, talk to everyone. Trying to get better at that, and not just be in a hurry the whole time. I am always in a hurry and trying to figure out how to do things faster so the Lord is teaching me patience. I think about how much patience the Lord has to have with us, His imperfect servants, and it helps me to have more patience with others.

"Love you all! I know that this gospel is true, and that it changes lives every day if we let it."

Does the Lord open doors? Do you believe He can open doors? Do you believe He wants you to do this work and you can do it? I believe the Lord wants this gospel taught so badly that He will do 90% of the work, if we will do just 10%, in faith.

Sister C. (Utah Provo Mission, 2012-2013):

December 24, 2013—"We'd had families inviting us to their Christmas Eve dinners all week long, and we weren't sure why but we turned down every dinner invitation we received. Around 1:00 in the afternoon a member of the High Council texted us and asked if we wanted to join him and his family. He told us there would be quite a few non-member and less-active members there. We accepted the invitation and when we got to his home we tried to talk to everyone and focus on missionary opportunities.

"Once we started eating we sat down next to a man named Aram and his mother. They were from the Middle Eastern country Jordan. Aram was attending college in Utah and his mother was visiting. Aram shared that he'd had a few missionary discussions since being here. He had quite a few different views and opinions that he started sharing with us. I listened and was polite, but I shared my testimony at every possible opportunity. The mother listened to our conversation very intently, and I could see in her eyes that she was recognizing truth. I know she felt the Spirit. She nodded her head as we testified of Christ and prophets and eternal families.

FIND "The High Council member asked if we wanted to share a message later on and we were grateful he gave us the opportunity. I excused myself for a minute, went into the bathroom and got on my knees to ask for help. I know we were at that dinner for a reason and we needed inspiration for what to share. I also prayed for the faith I needed to receive my answer. We shared a scripture and testified of the Savior. The Spirit filled the room and we were guided in every word that we said.

"We started to say goodbye and I felt that we needed to give Aram's mother a Book of Mormon. *TEACH* We ran out to the car and we only had one left, we went back inside and said to this woman, 'I know you have your religion. But this book will change your life. It's changed mine and I promise you it's true.' I continued to testify of the Book of Mormon and I could feel how important that interaction was. I felt a love for her that I can't explain. She accepted the Book of Mormon and said she would read it. She was planning to go back to Jordan about two weeks later. That night the High Council member texted us and said, 'Thank you for coming over tonight. I felt prompted to invite you this afternoon and I'm glad you were available.'"

FIND Elder A. asked me to assist his companionship with the teaching of Mr. P., a minister of the Hungarian Reformed Church. Upon leaving for the appointment, I commenced to pray about my role in the discussion. I was impressed that he would ask me about two questions: "Why should he submit himself to being taught by these two young men who were not schooled or trained in religion as he had been," and "How would he manage his affairs if he joined the Church and lost his income as a minister?" I pondered these feelings and thought about scriptures that might help resolve these concerns (Doctrine and Covenants 100:4-6).

Upon arriving at the home in Covina, California, the Elders and I were graciously received. After the prayer, *TEACH* the Elders began to teach the fourth discussion, and I listened and enjoyed their presentation. Suddenly, Mr. P. turned to me and stated, "I am a trained and ordained Iman. Why should I submit myself to being taught by these two young men who are not trained in theology as I have been?" I marveled at the question and proceeded to review a scripture that had been on my mind earlier during the drive to the appointment. I used Ephesians 4:11 as to offices in the Priesthood of God to do the work of preaching the gospel of Jesus Christ. He seemed satisfied with the explanation, and the Elders proceeded with the discussion. In a few moments, he again turned to me and asked, "If I join this Church, how will I manage my life and obtain an income, for I will be forced to give up my ministry?" Again I thought of the prompting received earlier. I called upon the scripture in John 15:16 wherein Jesus told His disciples "to go forth in faith," and trust in the Lord to open the door, to move forward and have the blessings you need. Satisfied, he asked the Elders to proceed, and they concluded the discussion.

BAPTIZE Several days later, Elder A. called me and asked if I was available on Saturday morning at 11:00. "Brother P. would like you to attend his baptism." Surely our Father in Heaven had a work for him to do in another place where his faith was fully recognized.

In the April 2020 General Conference, Sister Bonnie Cardon, Young Women General President spoke about having the light of Christ. She stated: "You and I have enough light to share right now. We can light the next step to help someone draw nearer to Jesus Christ, and then the next step, and the next" (General Conference, April 2020). Thus we can help gather Israel. The Lord will help magnify every small effort.

Sister C., Alabama Birmingham Mission, 2012-2013:

"We have had a lot going on and this week flew by! We helped do a church tour on Tuesday which was really fun, helping people learn a little bit more about our Church—and we did a musical number (we do a lot of those, but we have amazing sisters who can sing really well so it really brings the Spirit). Sister S. and I are having a lot of fun—we are a lot alike and the oldest child and so we have fun giving and taking—usually her ideas really are better than mine. We had some really neat experiences this week:

- *FIND* Met a part-member family—and the mom wants to know more about the Church because two religions are dividing her family, and she wants to know which one is the right one—we are so excited to work with her.

- *FIND* We were led to meet another lady and her two cute kids—she had a lot of questions and

- *TEACH* we taught her about the basics of the Church and introduced her to the Book of Mormon and it all made sense to her! We are looking forward to teaching her more—we clicked right away and she is so great, her daughter is 18-months old and we had fun trying to entertain her during the lesson too—the Spirit was so strong, and we are excited to see what happens in the coming week.

- We also had a great day on Saturday—all the things we had planned didn't feel 'right' so we kind of changed up the day and did service for members, visited investigators with cookies, and while we were doing *FIND* this we happened to run into a man who had a lot of extra canned goods, and we happened to be on our way to give other supplies to a family in need—it was such a neat experience—the Lord's hand was in it all!

"We have some good trainings coming up this week—President helps us a lot to keep us focused, and how we can become better missionaries.

"We are meeting a lot of great people, and getting the message of mormon.org out there— which makes it fun to talk and meet new people.

TEACH "Sister S. and I are starting to realize how to teach the people better to their needs. The first principle that we teach is that God is our loving Heavenly Father—He loves us so much He sent His Son, Jesus Christ, to go through everything we would so we could make it through this life with His help, and make it back to the next, only through Him! He is our help and advocate with the Father, we only need Him! He is everywhere in the Book of Mormon—that is the sole purpose of it, to help others understand their relationship with Christ and with our Father in Heaven. That is what we are here to figure out, and that is what we are here to do—to help others come unto Christ. I am thankful for the little lessons, inspiration, and help my companion gives me."

The double-doctor M. family—Mariana was a psychologist, and Philipi, was an M.D. Mariana and her daughter had joined the Church in San Marino, California, a year before we arrived in the California Arcadia Mission. FIND Judith and I became acquainted with them immediately through activities and socials with members. The Pasadena California Stake Mission President and I visited their home several times TEACH. Using several principles of "helping others feel and recognize the spirit," we challenged the doctor to be baptized on April 17! (He said that he laughed in his heart at that absurd proposal!) As we prepared to leave, a knock came at his door, and his wife opened it to find two of our missionaries. They were surprised to see that the Mission President was already there! The doctor made arrangements for the missionaries to visit three times in the following week. I returned a few days later with the Stake President, as my companion. We prayed, sang, bore testimony, expressed our love, etc., and were assured that progress was being made.

In the meantime, the two members were experiencing great turmoil in their lives through persecution in many forms. Mariana called and expressed alarm at the seriousness of the events. BAPTIZE I assured her that all would be well and her husband was going to be baptized. The Elders completed the discussions on schedule, and Philipi called me mid-week to invite me to participate in his baptism on April 17. The following week he was ordained, received a call as a stake missionary with his wife, and moved forward beautifully. I shall never forget the Lord's hand in this baptism. Words of faith were expressed with authority, and the man's heart was softened Several months after the baptism, I called this dear brother and invited him to say a prayer at a special Latin fireside. He declined. I was dismayed and repeated my request. He responded, "I cannot be at the fireside that evening. President, I am going to be with my wife at our first temple preparation class."

FIND Elder M. and I called on the R. family In West Covina, California one evening to teach the first discussion to three children. *TEACH* At the conclusion of the lesson, I asked the mother and the children how they felt about the things they had learned. Sensing their sincerity about the gospel, I asked the Elder if he had a question for them before we left. "Do you think we should ask them about a baptism date, Elder?" I asked. *BAPTIZE* He discussed a baptismal date for two weeks hence and had the privilege of performing the ordinance as scheduled.

FIND On November 29, I joined the Priesthood leaders of the Covina California Stake to make missionary home visits. Bishop B. and I were assigned Mike's family. His wife had joined the Church many years previously. Her Catholic husband had never had the discussions, though he was quite supportive of her Church involvement. As the Bishop and I visited with Mike, there was a sweet spirit of love and acceptance in the room. *TEACH* We discussed the principles of the gospel and their eternal impact upon him and his wife. In conclusion, I challenged Mike to hear the discussions from the missionaries, and to my great joy, he accepted the challenge. Over the next three months he worked his way toward baptism. *BAPTIZE* In mid-February, he called and invited me to speak at his baptismal service. What a joyous couple attended the sacred ordinance that Sunday evening. The chapel was filled as friends and saints witnessed this glorious event. Seventy-two-year-old Mike was now beginning a new life with his dear companion.

FIND My companion and I had visited a beautiful family as ministers for six years. Mother and young adult daughter were super active in the Church. The husband and father had not been a participant in the Church for many years. *TEACH* Always the visits were full of hope, love, caring, and invitations. Our family moved from the city and our regular contacts with this family ceased. Others carried on in my place.

Some 23 years later, my wife and I were on a Church assignment to that area (Spokane, Washington) once again. Following our participation in the conference with 1000's of members of the Church, the leader of the session took me aside and said, "Elder Coleman we have arranged for a family you know to meet with you for a few minutes now. Please come with me to where they are waiting." *BAP-TIZE* There they were! Husband and wife, children and their spouses. Brother M. embraced me. "We just wanted you to know that all of your years of visits to us were not in vain. We have been to the temple to be sealed and we are all participating in callings and service as members of the Church. Thank you so much for not giving up on us!" (Even as I write this now, I am brought to tears again, joyful tears, as I was when I saw this dear family again.) There is great joy in inviting them in or inviting them back!

FIND Elder T. and I called on the E. family as I had met them previously at a Glendora California Stake Conference. Their son was serving a full-time mission, but they were not members of the Church. *TEACH* We sang, read scriptures, prayed, bore testimony, and had a sweet visit. A sick grandchild was present, and Sister E. asked if there was something we could do for her. Elder T. and I blessed her, and marvelous healing took place that evening. We returned again and again over the period of several months, found Brother E. a job, gave his wife a blessing to assist with a word of wisdom problem, and served them with our faith and prayers.

BAPTIZE What a joyous day it was when Brother E. called and proclaimed that he and his wife were ready for baptism. It was a special time for many who had labored with this fine couple for many years.

FIND Marty came to a Mission President's Fireside. A former nun in the Catholic Church, she was full of questions about the restored gospel. *TEACH* Elder B. worked with her and encouraged her with mighty faith. She and I had several visits, and she told me an incredible story of faith and devotion as she served in her church. The gospel plan was a powerful magnet to her elect soul, *BAPTIZE* and her baptism was a joyous event. Sister Marty was home at last in the Lord's true Church.

As was a frequent occurrence, Sister Coleman and I were at the Methodist Hospital in Arcadia with Elder L. and Elder B. Elder L. had just broken bones in his hand in a bicycle accident, and was being attended to in the emergency room. *FIND* After some time, I was in the pharmacy to secure medication for the Elder, when I met Carla, a nurse at the hospital, who stopped briefly at the pharmacy also. Obtaining her name and address and noting her interest in our work, *TEACH* we sent the same two elders to her family shortly thereafter. Her husband was quick to put a stop to any further visits to their home. The family name went into the back of the missionaries' area book, and two years went by.

When I arrived home late one evening, Judith said, "You need to call this number." I protested, noting the lateness of the hour. She assured me it was okay and necessary. *BAPTIZE* "This is Carla," the lady responded. "You probably don't remember our meeting at the hospital several years ago!" Memories flooded back. "I just thought you would like to know, President Coleman. We are a little slow, but my husband and I and our two boys will be baptized next Sunday evening!" What a special evening indeed, as this great family entered the waters of baptism.

The Lord can work sweet miracles through all of us. Here is another example of an ordinary day, an ordinary place, and an extraordinary opportunity to find a child of God in need.

Sister L. (Brazil Florianopolis Mission, 2009-2011):

"My mission president asked us to try and teach more men. As a sister missionary this was quite intimidating, but we made a goal to contact at least two men a day. One Sunday the streets were empty and all appointments had fallen through. *FIND* We found ourselves at a park and we walked past a man sitting alone on a bench. Trying to avoid him, then we look at each other and knew we needed to do our part. So we approached him, his eyes were bloodshot and trembling. We told him we were representatives of Jesus Christ and he broke down sobbing right there in the park. Gelson began to tell us that we were an answer to a prayer at that moment. He had just been kicked out of three bars for drinking too much and was contemplating what to do with his life. We let him vent, got his information and invited him to a baptism that night. *TEACH* He ended up coming to the baptism! How he drove himself there, I don't know as he was still a bit drunk. He was so touched by the baptism that he wanted us to teach him more.

"Long story short, Gelson ended up leaving his at-the-time girlfriend he lived with and stopped drinking within a week of the first lesson. *BAPTIZE* He was baptized, received the priesthood, held callings, married a fabulous woman in the temple and we keep in touch on Facebook. He still thanks me for bringing the gospel to him and changing his life. Gelson is a classic example of not judging a book by its cover. We have to take the time to get to know each other and not be quick to judge."

12

Seek Joy With the Lord

Elder Dieter F. Uchtdorf, Quorum of the Twelve Apostles and Sister Harriet Uchtdorf—February 25, 2021:

"In the missionary devotional posted Thursday, February 25, on the missionaries' online portal, Elder Uchtdorf—who chairs the Church's Missionary Executive Council—saluted the elders and sisters of the COVID-19 pandemic era as those who learned to use technology and social media in new and effective ways to proclaim the gospel worldwide.

"'When restrictions to our missionary work ease again, don't just go back to the old ways. Go back to the future,' he said. 'Move forward and upward as you apply what you have learned during the pandemic.'

"Elder Uchtdorf said the Lord was not surprised by the pandemic. 'He prepared us and the world. He prepared the means and the tools. But it is up to you to discover these tools and use them effectively and efficiently in the Lord's way. You are engaged in *FINDING* and *TEACHING* methods that are dramatically different from the past.'

"Elder Uchtdorf promised that through trusting the Lord, the missionaries will find, teach and make disciples as they 'gather the seekers'—no matter the age, language, nationality, ethnicity, religious or socioeconomic background. 'With the help of technology,' he added, 'people might even find you.'

"Elder Uchtdorf said missionaries' social media products and technology efforts don't need to be perfect or professional, but rather authentic and intentional. *BAPTIZE* 'Use your heart when creating them, think of the people they are meant for, and seek the help of the Spirit. If you aim for these goals, I promise you the Spirit will help you to touch the hearts and the minds of the people.'

"Sister Uchtdorf told the missionaries, 'Your message brings the answers to life's most important questions to God's children. Life did not begin with birth, and it does not end with death. Families can be forever. Your very personal experiences applied to your message will bring peace and hope to all you will teach, and to you.'

"She recalled being a young girl in Frankfurt, Germany, watching her father suffer in the final weeks of his life and praying for help and comfort. *FIND* After his passing, 'this heavenly help finally came' as two missionaries knocked on the family's door, seeking to share the message of the restored gospel with the young, single-parent family. *TEACH*

"'It was as if angels had been sent to us from Heaven. The light they shared with us was the light of their testimonies, their love for the Lord and for us,' she said.

"Sister Uchtdorf reminded the missionaries that they are messengers of light, truth, glory, hope and happiness. 'Your daily service will bless many lives around you, *BAPTIZE* and I promise it also will bless you—with peace, hope, and a strong faith to move forward and upward'" (Scott Taylor, *Church News*, February 27, 2021).

Two years ago, we invited a group of our returned missionaries to our home for a fireside chat. *FIND* Elder S. and his wife brought with them Mr. and Mrs. L., the parents of his wife. As we shared the gospel with each other, we felt the family was touched also.

Sure enough, Sister L., a member of the Church all her life, *TEACH* invited her husband to read the literature I had provided him and receive the missionary discussions. *BAPTIZE* Judith and I were invited to attend his baptism recently and rejoice with this beautiful family in the blessings of the gospel! Soon there will be a sealing ordinance for them in the temple!

FIND What an experience Elder S. and I had that evening as we taught Jamie and Joe. *TEACH* "You cannot be baptized, Jamie, unless you no longer live with Joe. You must be married or you cannot live together." A tough stand; a no-compromising situation; but the Lord's way prevailed. A happy young adult followed counsel, a singles ward rallied around her, *BAPTIZE* a baptism was accomplished, and another soul entered the straight and narrow path.

FIND Judith and I met Lisa at a LaVerne California Stake Conference. *TEACH* We visited with her several times afterward and helped her resolve concerns. We encouraged the missionaries to be patient with her and understand her struggles. *BAPTIZE* How happy she is as a beautiful Church member! The gospel is for all of Father's children.

FIND The Elders persuaded an old gentleman to attend a special fireside in the La Crescenta California Stake Center. *TEACH* President and Sister Coleman were speaking and greeting the guests. Following the fireside, Joe related to the missionaries how his heart had been touched, *BAPTIZE* and he wanted to be baptized. Is anything too hard for the Lord?

FIND The fireside at the bishop's home that Sunday evening was attended by many members and one beautiful Latin young adult. *TEACH* I bore my testimony specifically to her on several instances during the course of the evening. As I was partaking of punch and cookies before leaving the bishop's home, one of the elders said that Maria wished to speak to me privately. Our conversation was centered upon her feelings during the fireside. *BAPTIZE* "I felt your message was true," she said, "and I want the missionaries to teach me that I may be prepared and join the Church!" The Lord truly blesses his servants who seek to bear witness of his restored gospel.

FIND I shall always remember the petite Latin teller at the bank I frequented in Arcadia, California. *TEACH* Talking about the gospel at the teller window is a challenge, but she was always so receptive.

"What's this, you have a boyfriend, Carina? When are you going to join the Church?"

"No way," she responded. "I'm a Catholic. My family will never accept that happening." I talked of the temple, slipped literature to her, planted seeds of faith, time after time. She married, she moved, and I wondered what happened to her. Sister M. called me one day and said she was teaching a young woman who was married to a fine Church member. I enquired as to her name. "Her name is Carina." My heart jumped! Could it be my friend of two years, Carina? I asked Sister M. to inquire if she used to work in Arcadia, California at the bank. *BAPTIZE* Word came back that Carina was my golden bank teller, and her baptism into the Covina Spanish Branch was met with excitement by all the members. I saw her a few weeks ago. Her husband is in the Elder's Quorum Presidency and Carina is serving as the Relief Society Secretary. "Oh yes," she said, "we are going to the temple as soon as I have been in the Church one year." I still shed tears of joy when I think of her growth and development and faith to join the Church.

FIND I noticed a young father standing uncomfortably near the stage, holding a small child. The Spirit prompted me to speak with him. He was there with his wife and daughter and son. He was a less-active member, and his wife, Beatrice, was not a member. "Are we out of place?" he inquired, as his concern showed regarding their dress for the evening. The members were in Sunday garb, and he and his wife were more casual. "This meeting is for you," I assured him. "You are just fine and most welcome." *TEACH* Escorting them to the chapel for the presentation, Judith and I then proceeded to speak at the Covina California Stake fireside for prospective members. We were followed by the viewing of the video "Together Forever." As the video began in the darkened room, I heard the cry of a small child near the back of the chapel. I quickly moved to the mother. It was Beatrice with baby Daniel. I asked if I could hold him while the video was shown. She felt Daniel would not come to me, as he had never let anyone hold him before. "You need to hear the message of this film," I assured her. "Daniel and I will be just fine." I held the little one for the next half hour, and we conversed in the celestial language of tiny spirits one year from a heavenly home. The mother walked out in the foyer following the video and rejoiced that Daniel and I were doing just fine.

BAPTIZE At her baptism three weeks later, Beatrice thanked us again for the opportunity to feel the spirit of the Lord that evening and the unusual experience the Mission President had with Daniel. A simple act of service to a young mother and child provided the opportunity for the gospel to be planted in a grateful heart. Surely we shall rejoice with this "sheave" forever!

So many times our finding and teaching experiences are very close to our normal every day living. We just need to seek the Lord's direction for the new occasion to help.

Elder J. (Chile Santiago North Mission, 2015-2017):

"Yolanda was a devout member of The Church of Jesus Christ of Latter-day Saints and she attended faithfully every week. Her husband, Humberto, and her daughter, Fabiola, a young adult, were not members of the Church. Yolanda yearned for her family to receive the blessings of the gospel. *FIND* She had on many occasions invited the missionaries into their home to teach her family. Elder R. and I knew of this and we were inspired to go in with a new approach.

"When we would go to their home, Humberto was always there but Fabiola was always away at school and work, so we rarely saw her. The Spirit told us that Fabiola was the one who we needed to focus our efforts on. So, when we went into that home, we made an increased effort to invite Fabiola to participate in our lessons. We asked her for a time when she would be able to sit down and let us teach her.

"As we began to focus on Fabiola, we sought for revelation on what we needed to teach her as we know she had been taught many lessons from various missionaries in the past. As we studied and discussed together and prayed, we felt so inspired that we needed to start from the very beginning and teach about the restoration.

TEACH "During the following weeks, we proceeded to teach her all the lessons. Her biggest concerns were about Joseph Smith and the truthfulness of the Book of Mormon. We began to focus our efforts on committing her to read the Book of Mormon daily and pray to know of its truthfulness.

"Fabiola began to respond to the commitment. She started reading from the beginning page of the Book of Mormon. She was enjoying her reading and began praying. As we followed up with her, she said she had not received an answer yet, but we had faith and knew she would gain a witness.

"Fabiola continued progressing well, had been reading the Book of Mormon but still needed to pray to receive an answer. One day when we taught her, she told us that she would be baptized this week if she received an answer. We were excited for her and continued encouraging her to pray and ask so she would gain a witness of the truth.

"When she came upon 1st Nephi 4, she got kind of hung up on the story of Nephi being commanded to kill Laban. She thought: why would God command Nephi to break a commandment that He had already given? We explained the best we could, but she continued to struggle with that. She did, however, continue to act in faith as she continued to respond to our commitment challenges to read and pray about the Book of Mormon.

"The week of February 5, 2017 turned out great. On Tuesday we went and were planning to teach something from the Book of Mormon so that she could really learn the importance of gaining a testimony of the Book of Mormon and of Joseph Smith. We noticed she was kind of acting different when we got there. She was very quiet and not responding much. We asked her if she had been reading from the Book of Mormon and praying. *BAPTIZE* She answered, 'yes, and I want to get baptized this week, is that alright?' We were so happy. Our fasting and prayers had been answered. We responded 'yes' and then we made plans for her special baptism to take place on February 12th. We asked her how she got her answer. She said, she had prayed and opened the Book of Mormon to Alma 32 and received her answer.

"On Sunday, February 12th we had her baptism following church. It was a great baptism. We all felt the Holy Ghost's presence. One of the best parts of this baptism experience was that her dad, Humberto, showed up. He had said all week that he was not willing to come to Fabiola's baptism, but to our joy he showed up moments before the baptism service began and he really enjoyed it.

"Following the baptism, Humberto expressed to us that he was now open and willing to attend our church meetings. I really believe that he also will come into the waters of baptism someday. We just need to work with him and teach by the power of the Spirit so he will gain a witness that he needs to be baptized.

"I have faith and pray that Yolanda will have her desires to have all her family join her in the blessings of being members of The Church of Jesus Christ of Latter-day Saints. It was a tremendous blessing to be a part of the work to bring that family a step closer to a forever family."

FIND The C. family had been visited countless times. *TEACH* The Elders had even taught them all six discussions. But they had some serious concerns to resolve. The time for baptism faded away. Weeks turned into months. The Stake Mission President and I made repeated visits to their home. Next time—try again—come back later—no one home. President M. and I secured another appointment. We prayed, we expressed words of faith, we assured each other the Lord would help us. They were home! They were receptive! We boldly expressed the feelings of our hearts. "Brother and Sister C., the Lord loves you and will receive you into his Church. This is what you must do." We read scriptures together, prayed, bore testimony, reassured, encouraged, and committed them for baptism!

BAPTIZE "Could it be on the 21st or would it be okay on the 15th?" Her question thrilled us. The missionaries taught the lessons again, and the baptism of two special children of God was accomplished. The gospel changes lives, breaks down barriers, and renders old fears and concerns resolvable. This is a choice work.

FIND Elder L. called and asked, "President, can you help us teach a beautiful Catholic family here in Walnut, California? The father wants to talk to you because we told him you had been a Catholic." *TEACH* Brother N. and his family had been taught by the missionaries for many weeks. What a blessing it was for me to meet this choice family; father, mother, one son, and two daughters. How sincere they were about their lessons and growth in the gospel. It was clear to me that Brother Latin was a man of faith and very concerned about leading his family in righteousness. *BAPTIZE* It was such a joy to see him lead his family by being baptized first. In just a few days, he was ordained and shortly thereafter he baptized his wife and children.

I know that friendshipping and fellowshipping are powerful missionary tools. When I was a prospective member, a returned missionary friend never ceased to be interested in my activities. I played college baseball and I can remember dozens of times when my Mormon friend would visit practices and watch until he caught my eye. He would share a few words of encouragement and show an interest in me. Soon he sought me out on other occasions and shared his friendship with me. When I attended my first non-Catholic Sunday School class (after Catholic mass of course), I was made welcome by this good brother. Later, as I committed myself to learn more about the gospel, this man was, again, my teacher. My decision to join the Church was finalized in his home in a cottage meeting setting. My friend baptized me. Over the years I have cherished his efforts to fellowship me. His friendship was a key to bringing me the gospel.

So, where do we start? We start where we are! That is what happened in the following example.

Elder L. (New York New York South Mission, 2012-2014):

"It was a sunny afternoon in Flushing, New York. I was busily handing out flyers for our missionary-led English class when a man with a thick northeastern Chinese accent snatched a slip from my hand. He belligerently asked who organized the classes. I responded, 'The Church of Jesus Christ of Latter-day Saints." *FIND* He seemed to perk up as I mentioned church and rattled off more queries, 'Are you a true church?' 'Do you worship Jesus Christ?'

'Do you read the Bible?' I invited Steven to meet with us for a more comprehensive discussion about the gospel. He agreed to meet. A couple of days later, my companion and I were sitting in the church foyer waiting for Steven to arrive when we received a phone call. Steven was on his way, but he had accidentally gone into the wrong church a block down the street. The priest at the other church advised Steven to avoid our 'false doctrine.' Steven was understandably confused, but we managed to convince him to meet with us for a half hour. TEACH He came. We sat down to teach the first lesson. He spoke with a raised, combative voice but his questions were sincere. As the lesson progressed, his demeanor softened. We showed him the video of the first vision. The aggression he emanated coming into the discussion evaporated. He wanted to learn more. BAPTIZE We continued teaching Steven for another six weeks before he was baptized. Today he is still an active member of the Flushing Ward and is one of the friendliest people I worked with as a missionary.

It is not necessary to focus formally on the "I bear you my testimony ... " phrase or the use of "I know ..." in every sentence we use to explain our feelings about the gospel. That can be overdone and therefore ineffective. There are many ways to express our testimony which are natural and concise and part of our normal communication.

Perhaps an illustration of the power of testimony will help explain this important principle. FIND One evening as I prepared to teach an Institute of Religion class, a young woman entered the room with Church friends. I introduced myself to her and learned that she was a Catholic girl who was single. I welcomed her and she took a seat on the back row. At the end of the class, I looked at her and indicated to her personally (though sixty other persons were present in the room) the truthfulness of the gospel. When she came up to me after class I told her, "We would be pleased to have you come again. We appreciate you being with us." She said, "Well, maybe I will come back."

TEACH The next week she did come back. Again, she sat on the back row. Toward the end of class, I again looked at her and bore testimony of what had been taught that evening. Then I asked if anyone had any questions. This Catholic girl raised her hand. BAPTIZE "I just had a strange feeling come over me," she said. "I feel I am going to join this Church!" That "strange" feeling!

The profound power of testimony through the-Holy Ghost strikes deep into the soul. A heart is changed. She had experienced what Moroni had promised when he wrote, "by the power of the Holy Ghost ye may know the truth of all things" (Moroni 10:5). Three weeks after this experience she was baptized.

Testimony Helps Spiritual Conversion

As we bear testimony of the truth, the Holy Ghost may manifest or witness to the person we are addressing that what we have said is, indeed, true. We thus provide an opportunity for a spiritual manifestation for that person.

The conversion process is very personal. When accompanied by spiritual promptings and feelings, the convert is assured of a much greater opportunity for joining the Church for the right reasons. He will join because of his love for Christ and a desire to follow His commandments. Neither we nor the missionaries "convert" anyone; the Holy Ghost is the conversion influence. As President Kimball has testified: "The power of conversion is directly associated with the Holy Ghost, for no person can be truly converted and know that Jesus is the Christ save by the power of the Holy Ghost."

The gospel of Jesus Christ is true. We enjoy the blessing of belonging to the only true Church upon the face of the whole earth. Jesus Christ is our Savior and it is His work which we share with others. We are led by living prophets who teach and expound the restored gospel! I know the Book of Mormon is true for I have received the witness promised by Moroni. Joseph Smith was indeed a prophet of God. May we sincerely pray that the Lord will help us share the gospel with family and friends. May we bear testimony to those whom we fellowship that we have a precious gift which will change their lives and bring them great joy.

I have woven together sixty years of missionary experiences illustrated through the fundamental foundations of finding, teaching and baptizing our Father's children from any place, any time and in any circumstances they may be found. Imagine my joy in recent weeks, when Elder and Sister Uchtdorf brought these principles to the forefront in their missionary devotional across the globe!

I have shared missionary success stories over the past 60 years from my wife and I, my brother and his grandsons, my sister and her grandchildren, our sons and grandsons, granddaughters, grand-nephews, local ward members, and local missionaries serving in our ward. Our oldest daughter and her husband are serving a mission in the Philippines where he is a mission president and she is his missionary companion. This span of time and experiences touch many missions of the world. As my brother and sister and I have been gathered to Israel, our family members continue to gather even more of our Father's precious children to Israel through the blessed restored gospel of Jesus Christ. We have seen success from teaching formal missionary discussions, to more open-ended lessons as to needs of those being taught, to electronic influence in finding, preparing to teach, and follow up from country to country!

May the Lord continue to bless this worldwide effort to gather Israel to the Restored Gospel of Jesus Christ and bring the everlasting joy of this holy work to more and more of His beloved children in these latter days.

Appendix I

Mormon Messages on YouTube—February 2009
Elder Gary J. Coleman, of the Seventy

G rowing up in my family, we lived as devout members of another Christian faith. I was baptized a member of that church
shortly after my birth. Our family went to church each week. I
thought that someday I would enter the full-time ministry in my
church. There was no question in our minds that we could define
ourselves as devout Christians.

When I was a university student, however, I became acquainted with the members and teachings of The Church of Jesus Christ
of Latter-day Saints, a Christian faith centered on the Savior. I began to learn about the doctrine of the Restoration of the gospel
of Jesus Christ in these latter days. I learned truths that I had not
known before that changed my life and how I viewed the gospel.

The first restored truth that I learned was the nature of the Godhead. It was a stunning awakening for me to finally understand
the truth about the nature of God the Eternal Father and His Only
Begotten Son.

The second restored truth I learned as an investigator of this
Church was the reality of additional scripture and revelation. The
prophet Isaiah saw in vision a book that he proclaimed was part
of "a marvellous work and a wonder!"[1] I testify that the Book of
Mormon: Another Testament of Jesus Christ is that book.

I first read the Book of Mormon at the age of 21. I then asked
God if it was true. The truth of it was manifested unto me by the
comforting power of the Holy Ghost.[2] I know that the Book of
Mormon is a second testament of Jesus Christ.

Another restored truth of the gospel I became acquainted with
was the restoration of priesthood authority, or the power to act in

---

1. See Isaiah 29:11-12, 14, 18.
2. See Moroni 10:4-5.

God's name. Former prophets and apostles, such as Elijah, Moses, John the Baptist, Peter, James, and John, have been sent by God and Christ in our day to restore the holy priesthood of God. Every priesthood holder in this Church can trace his priesthood authority directly to Jesus Christ.

I am a devout Christian who is exceedingly fortunate to have this greater knowledge and blessing in my life since my conversion to the restored Church. And, I testify of these truths in the name of Jesus Christ, amen.

Truth has been restored.

1. See Isaiah 29:11-12, 14, 18.
2. See Moroni 10:4-5.

THE LIVING CHRIST

THE TESTIMONY OF THE APOSTLES

THE CHURCH OF JESUS CHRIST OF LATTER-DAY SAINTS

As we commemorate the birth of Jesus Christ two millennia ago, we offer our testimony of the reality of His matchless life and the infinite virtue of His great atoning sacrifice. None other has had so profound an influence upon all who have lived and will yet live upon the earth.

He was the Great Jehovah of the Old Testament, the Messiah of the New. Under the direction of His Father, He was the creator of the earth. "All things were made by him; and without him was not any thing made that was made" (John 1:3). Though sinless, He was baptized to fulfill all righteousness. He "went about doing good" (Acts 10:38), yet was despised for it. His gospel was a message of peace and goodwill. He entreated all to follow His example. He walked the roads of Palestine, healing the sick, causing the blind to see, and raising the dead. He taught the truths of eternity, the reality of our premortal existence, the purpose of our life on earth, and the potential for the sons and daughters of God in the life to come.

He instituted the sacrament as a reminder of His great atoning sacrifice. He was arrested and condemned on spurious charges, convicted to satisfy a mob, and sentenced to die on Calvary's cross. He gave His life to atone for the sins of all mankind. His was a great vicarious gift in behalf of all who would ever live upon the earth.

We solemnly testify that His life, which is central to all human history, neither began in Bethlehem nor concluded on Calvary. He was the Firstborn of the Father, the Only Begotten Son in the flesh, the Redeemer of the world.

He rose from the grave to "become the firstfruits of them that slept" (1 Corinthians 15:20). As Risen Lord, He visited among those He had loved in life. He also ministered among His "other sheep" (John 10:16) in ancient America. In the modern world, He and His Father appeared to the boy Joseph Smith, ushering in the long-promised "dispensation of the fulness of times" (Ephesians 1:10).

Of the Living Christ, the Prophet Joseph wrote: "His eyes were as a flame of fire; the hair of his head was white like the pure snow; his countenance shone above the brightness of the sun; and his voice was as the sound of the rushing of great waters, even the voice of Jehovah, saying:

"I am the first and the last; I am he who liveth, I am he who was slain; I am your advocate with the Father" (D&C 110:3–4).

Of Him the Prophet also declared: "And now, after the many testimonies which have been given of him, this is the testimony, last of all, which we give of him: That he lives!

"For we saw him, even on the right hand of God; and we heard the voice bearing record that he is the Only Begotten of the Father—

"That by him, and through him, and of him, the worlds are and were created, and the inhabitants thereof are begotten sons and daughters unto God" (D&C 76:22–24).

We declare in words of solemnity that His priesthood and His Church have been restored upon the earth— "built upon the foundation of . . . apostles and prophets, Jesus Christ himself being the chief corner stone" (Ephesians 2:20).

We testify that He will someday return to earth. "And the glory of the Lord shall be revealed, and all flesh shall see it together" (Isaiah 40:5). He will rule as King of Kings and reign as Lord of Lords, and every knee shall bend and every tongue shall speak in worship before Him. Each of us will stand to be judged of Him according to our works and the desires of our hearts.

We bear testimony, as His duly ordained Apostles— that Jesus is the Living Christ, the immortal Son of God. He is the great King Immanuel, who stands today on the right hand of His Father. He is the light, the life, and the hope of the world. His way is the path that leads to happiness in this life and eternal life in the world to come. God be thanked for the matchless gift of His divine Son.

THE FIRST PRESIDENCY

[signatures]
Thomas S. Monson
James E. Faust

THE QUORUM OF THE TWELVE

[signatures]
Boyd K. Packer
L. Tom Perry
David B. Haight
Neal A. Maxwell
Russell M. Nelson
Dallin H. Oaks
M. Russell Ballard
Joseph B. Wirthlin
Richard G. Scott
Robert D. Hales
Jeffrey R. Holland
Henry B. Eyring

January 1, 2000

THE FAMILY

A PROCLAMATION TO THE WORLD

The First Presidency and Council of the Twelve Apostles of The Church of Jesus Christ of Latter-day Saints

WE, THE FIRST PRESIDENCY and the Council of the Twelve Apostles of The Church of Jesus Christ of Latter-day Saints, solemnly proclaim that marriage between a man and a woman is ordained of God and that the family is central to the Creator's plan for the eternal destiny of His children.

ALL HUMAN BEINGS—male and female—are created in the image of God. Each is a beloved spirit son or daughter of heavenly parents, and, as such, each has a divine nature and destiny. Gender is an essential characteristic of individual premortal, mortal, and eternal identity and purpose.

IN THE PREMORTAL REALM, spirit sons and daughters knew and worshipped God as their Eternal Father and accepted His plan by which His children could obtain a physical body and gain earthly experience to progress toward perfection and ultimately realize their divine destiny as heirs of eternal life. The divine plan of happiness enables family relationships to be perpetuated beyond the grave. Sacred ordinances and covenants available in holy temples make it possible for individuals to return to the presence of God and for families to be united eternally.

THE FIRST COMMANDMENT that God gave to Adam and Eve pertained to their potential for parenthood as husband and wife. We declare that God's commandment for His children to multiply and replenish the earth remains in force. We further declare that God has commanded that the sacred powers of procreation are to be employed only between man and woman, lawfully wedded as husband and wife.

WE DECLARE the means by which mortal life is created to be divinely appointed. We affirm the sanctity of life and of its importance in God's eternal plan.

HUSBAND AND WIFE have a solemn responsibility to love and care for each other and for their children. "Children are an heritage of the Lord" (Psalm 127:3). Parents have a sacred duty to rear their children in love and righteousness, to provide for their physical and spiritual needs, and to teach them to love and serve one another, observe the commandments of God, and be law-abiding citizens wherever they live. Husbands and wives—mothers and fathers—will be held accountable before God for the discharge of these obligations.

THE FAMILY is ordained of God. Marriage between man and woman is essential to His eternal plan. Children are entitled to birth within the bonds of matrimony, and to be reared by a father and a mother who honor marital vows with complete fidelity. Happiness in family life is most likely to be achieved when founded upon the teachings of the Lord Jesus Christ. Successful marriages and families are established and maintained on principles of faith, prayer, repentance, forgiveness, respect, love, compassion, work, and wholesome recreational activities. By divine design, fathers are to preside over their families in love and righteousness and are responsible to provide the necessities of life and protection for their families. Mothers are primarily responsible for the nurture of their children. In these sacred responsibilities, fathers and mothers are obligated to help one another as equal partners. Disability, death, or other circumstances may necessitate individual adaptation. Extended families should lend support when needed.

WE WARN that individuals who violate covenants of chastity, who abuse spouse or offspring, or who fail to fulfill family responsibilities will one day stand accountable before God. Further, we warn that the disintegration of the family will bring upon individuals, communities, and nations the calamities foretold by ancient and modern prophets.

WE CALL UPON responsible citizens and officers of government everywhere to promote those measures designed to maintain and strengthen the family as the fundamental unit of society.

This proclamation was read by President Gordon B. Hinckley as part of his message at the General Relief Society Meeting held September 23, 1995, in Salt Lake City, Utah.

Appendix IV

Book of Mormon Marking Guide

(Evidence the Book of Mormon is Another Testament of Jesus Christ)

Go to page(s):	Read verse(s)
21	27, 31, 33
59	25
73-75	13-15, 21-23, 28-29
109-110	3, 8
113-114	5, 17
115	9
116-117	10-11
151-153	5, 8, 17, 19
201	25-26
225	14-16
236	40-41
283-285	43-44, 49, 52, 60
289	17-18, 21, 26-27
295	32
308	11-14
377-378	9-12
403	30-31
428-430	8, 10, 22-26, 33-34
438	21-24
443	15-21

459-460	19-22
464	6-7
485-486	16-17, 19, 21
495	11-12
520	2-3
529	4-5
531	32-33

The missionaries will teach you how to pray. Ask God, with a sincere heart and faith in Christ, about the truth of the things you have read. Continue the lessons with the missionaries that you may know how to partake of the fullness of the restored gospel of Jesus Christ.

Appendix V

THE RESTORATION OF THE FULNESS OF THE GOSPEL OF JESUS CHRIST

A BICENTENNIAL PROCLAMATION TO THE WORLD

THE FIRST PRESIDENCY AND COUNCIL OF THE TWELVE APOSTLES OF THE CHURCH OF JESUS CHRIST OF LATTER-DAY SAINTS

We solemnly proclaim that God loves His children in every nation of the world. God the Father has given us the divine birth, the incomparable life, and the infinite atoning sacrifice of His Beloved Son, Jesus Christ. By the power of the Father, Jesus rose again and gained the victory over death. He is our Savior, our Exemplar, and our Redeemer.

Two hundred years ago, on a beautiful spring morning in 1820, young Joseph Smith, seeking to know which church to join, went into the woods to pray near his home in upstate New York, USA. He had questions regarding the salvation of his soul and trusted that God would direct him.

In humility, we declare that in answer to his prayer, God the Father and His Son, Jesus Christ, appeared to Joseph and inaugurated the "restitution of all things" (Acts 3:21) as foretold in the Bible. In this vision, he learned that following the death of the original Apostles, Christ's New Testament Church was lost from the earth. Joseph would be instrumental in its return.

We affirm that under the direction of the Father and the Son, heavenly messengers came to instruct Joseph and re-establish the Church of Jesus Christ. The resurrected John the Baptist restored the authority to baptize by immersion for the remission of sins. Three of the original twelve Apostles—Peter, James, and John—restored the apostleship and keys of priesthood authority. Others came as well, including Elijah, who restored the authority to join families together forever in eternal relationships that transcend death.

We further witness that Joseph Smith was given the gift and power of God to translate an ancient record: the Book of Mormon—Another Testament of Jesus Christ. Pages of this sacred text include an account of the personal ministry of Jesus Christ among people in the Western Hemisphere soon after His Resurrection. It teaches of life's purpose and explains the doctrine of Christ, which is central to that purpose. As a companion scripture to the Bible, the Book of Mormon testifies that all human beings are sons and daughters of a loving Father in Heaven, that He has a divine plan for our lives, and that His Son, Jesus Christ, speaks today as well as in days of old.

We declare that The Church of Jesus Christ of Latter-day Saints, organized on April 6, 1830, is Christ's New Testament Church restored. This Church is anchored in the perfect life of its chief cornerstone, Jesus Christ, and in His infinite Atonement and literal Resurrection. Jesus Christ has once again called Apostles and has given them priesthood authority. He invites all of us to come unto Him and His Church, to receive the Holy Ghost, the ordinances of salvation, and to gain enduring joy.

Two hundred years have now elapsed since this Restoration was initiated by God the Father and His Beloved Son, Jesus Christ. Millions throughout the world have embraced a knowledge of these prophesied events.

We gladly declare that the promised Restoration goes forward through continuing revelation. The earth will never again be the same, as God will "gather together in one all things in Christ" (Ephesians 1:10).

With reverence and gratitude, we as His Apostles invite all to know—as we do—that the heavens are open. We affirm that God is making known His will for His beloved sons and daughters. We testify that those who prayerfully study the message of the Restoration and act in faith will be blessed to gain their own witness of its divinity and of its purpose to prepare the world for the promised Second Coming of our Lord and Savior, Jesus Christ.

This proclamation was read by President Russell M. Nelson as part of his message at the 190th Annual General Conference, April 5, 2020, in Salt Lake City, Utah.

Appendix VI

Hymns Referencing Joy, Rejoice, Joyful

#3 Now Let Us Rejoice

"Let us rejoice in the day of salvation"

#9 Come, Rejoice

"Come, rejoice the King of Glory"
"Joyous Wondrous Strain"
"Sing, rejoice the King of Love"

#18 The Voice of God Again is Heard

"Rejoice, ye living and ye dead!"
"Rejoice, for your salvation begins anew"

#58 Come, Ye Children Of the Lord

"Let us raise a joyful strain"
"O how joyful it will be when our Savior we shall see!"
"We will shout in joyous lays!"
"Then with joy each heart shall swell"

#64 On This Day of Joy and Gladness

"On this day of joy and gladness"

#66 Rejoice, the Lord is King!

"Rejoice, the Lord is King!

#136 I Know That My Redeemer Lives

"Oh, sweet the joy this sentence gives: I know that my Redeemer lives!"

#147 Sweet is the Work

"When in the realms of joy I see, Thy face in full felicity"

#227 There is Sunshine in My Soul Today

"For joy's laid up above"

#243 Let Us All Press On

"Let us all press on in the work of the Lord,
That when life is o'er we may gain a reward;
In the fight for right let us wield a sword,
The mighty sword of truth.

We will not retreat, though our numbers may be few
When compared with the opposite host in view;
But an unseen pow'r will aid me and you
In the glorious cause of truth.

If we do what's right we have no need to fear,
For the Lord, our helper, will ever be near;
In the days of trial his Saints he will cheer,
And prosper the cause of truth.

Chorus:
Fear not, though the enemy deride;
Courage, for the Lord is on our side.
We will heed not what the wicked may say.
But the Lord alone we will obey."

#257 Rejoice! A Glorious Sound is Heard

"Send forth a joyous strain"

#275 Men are That They Might Have Joy

"Oh, men are that they might have joy"
"For, men are that they might have joy"

#294 Love at Home

There is joy in every sound, when there's love at home

About the Author

 Elder Gary J. Coleman was in college when he first heard about the message of the Restored Gospel, although he was a devout Christian and follower of Christ, the powerful message brought major changes for the better in his life.

Headed for the robes of the Catholic priesthood, this altar boy and would-be bishop became a family man and a General Authority in The Church of Jesus Christ of Latter-day Saints instead.

His Diocese Bishop, at an early age, assured him he would be a priest, and not only that, a Bishop. His family, and in particular, his beloved grandmother, encouraged him to prepare for the priesthood. His young classmates who entered the Seminary encouraged him to do so many times.

His numerous visits with parish priests to established Seminaries over the course of his youth hastened his desire to become a priest. His service as an altar boy on a weekly basis over a twelve year period were constant opportunities to ponder upon full-time service in the church. His involvement in the Catholic Youth Organization (CYO) and as an instructor in catechism classes encouraged him to enter the work of the ministry. His family was named the diocese Catholic Family of the Year and his vision of entering the full time priesthood kept growing.

Elder Coleman was baptized in 1962. Since that time, he has been in five full time mission presidencies and served as president of the California Arcadia Mission, 1987-90, and as president of the New York Rochester Mission in the spring of 1998.

An educator by profession, Elder Coleman taught in the Church Educational System for 28 years. He was associate director of the Institute of Religion at Weber State University in Ogden, Utah at the time of his call to serve as a full-time General Authority of the Church in 1992. He was given General Authority Emeritus status in October 2011.

Elder Coleman earned his undergraduate degree at Washington State University. He also holds both a master's degree of education in counseling and guidance, and a doctorate degree in educational psychology from Brigham Young University.

He is married to Judith England Coleman. They are the parents of six children and have nineteen grandchildren and five great grandchildren.

It is his desire to share his experience with others especially investigators, new converts and missionaries, so that they too might experience the same joys and satisfaction that have attended him and his family since becoming affiliated with The Church of Jesus Christ of Latter-day Saints.